A Chef for All Seasons

A Practical, Two-Week Macrobiotic
Menu Plan with 37 Time-Saving
Cooking Ideas

Diane Avoli
Foreword by Aveline Kushi

One Peaceful World Press
Becket, Massachusetts

A Chef for All Seasons
© 1999 by Diane Avoli

All rights reserved. Printed in the United States of America. No part of this book may be used or reproduced in any manner whatsoever without written permission except in the case of brief quotations embodied in critical articles or reviews. For information, contact the publisher.

For further information on mail-order sales, wholesale or retail discounts, distribution, translations, and foreign rights, please contact the publisher:

One Peaceful World Press
P.O. Box 10
Leland Road
Becket, MA 01223
U.S.A.

Telephone (413) 623-2322
Fax (413) 623-6042

First Edition: June 1999

10 9 8 7 6 5 4 3 2 1

ISBN 1-882984-36-6
Printed in U.S.A.

Foreword

Diane Avoli has taught macrobiotic and natural foods cooking for over twenty-five years. She has been one of the most popular cooking teachers at the Kushi Institute, the annual Summer Conference, and the K.I. Extension Program in New York, Cleveland, San Francisco, Toronto, and other cities throughout North America. Over the years, I have found her food to be tasty and energizing and her techniques clear and simple. As the mother of eight children, she has been responsible for cooking for a large family every day. Thanks to her wonderful food, everyone in her family has enjoyed excellent health and is well the way to realizing his or her dream.

A Chef for All Seasons, Diane's first cookbook, presents over 150 delicious whole foods dishes made with whole grains, beans and bean products, vegetables from land and sea, and the highest quality natural sweeteners.

The complete two-week menu plan in this book features a cornucopia of delicious, healthful recipes such as: Amasake Smoothie, Apple Fritters, Carrot Soup, Homemade Rice Kayu Bread, Millet Loaf, Mochi Pancakes, Nori Rolls, Pressed Salad, Rice with Black Soybeans, Seitan with Apricot Sauce, Tempura, and Tofu Lasagna.

In these pages, Diane shows you how to change the seasoning, modify the flame or cooking time, and make other simple adjustments. The balanced menus and clear, step-by-step recipes in Diane's book can easily be adapted throughout the year. In this way, you too can become a chef for all seasons and create health and happiness.

> Aveline Kushi
> Brookline, Massachusetts
> February 27, 1999

Introduction

This book has been designed for those just starting the great adventure of macrobiotics as well as for those who have been exploring this way of life for a while.

The book presents two weeks of menus, including basic dishes, unusual dishes, and information on short cuts, uses for leftovers, and suggestions for changing dishes to satisfy individual needs within a household. Also included are recipes for making pickles and condiments, homemade steamed bread, and seitan.

Seasonal changes are important to keep us in balance with our environment. For colder weather we turn to heartier dishes, larger pieces of vegetables cooked longer, and more energizing methods of cooking. Warmer weather calls for lighter cooking styles and seasonal vegetables. The dishes in this book can be easily adapted to the weather by the choice of ingredients, length of cooking time, and styles of preparation.

The recipes should be read—and ideally prepared—from the start, beginning with Day 1 of Week 1, as the directions are reduced as the days go by in order not to repeat basic steps such as how to prepare wakame for miso soup. Pickle recipes should be prepared ahead of time.

I hope the reader enjoys these recipes as I have presented them, but my real wish is that they be a springboard for developing creativity and intuition. Everyone is different, their life experiences are unique, and their cooking should ultimately reflect their own creative art.

Thank you, Laura Wepman, for your encouragement and help with editing.

Diane Avoli
East Templeton, Massachusetts
February 21, 1999

Time-Saving Cooking Ideas

Cooking Grains

1. Prepare enough rice and other grains for more than one meal or day. Use extra for breakfast cereal, lunch, or as a second grain for the second day's dinner, as in a rice salad or soup. Remember that reheating is creating more yang (tightening, contracting) energy.
2. Combine a quick cooking grain, or processed grain, with a small amount of leftover grain to stretch it for a cereal or salad such as oatmeal or couscous.
3. Older grain could be used up in a grain pudding, rice kayu bread, or to make amasake, even if the grain contains beans or vegetables.
4. Plan your meals ahead so you know what days you will need time to cook whole grain. Planning ahead will help you to keep variety in your grains.
5. Long time cooking of whole grains for breakfast cereals can be prepared the day before. Wash and soak grain (e.g., barley and whole oats) in the morning, cook in the evening while eating dinner or cleaning up, store overnight, and heat for breakfast the next morning. Make extra to use in a dinner or lunch soup.
6. Use noodles, processed grain, or bread for your grain part of the meal once in a while when there is no time to cook a whole grain.
7. Remember that unroasted boiled millet usually only takes about 30 minutes to prepare; roasted, 25 minutes or less.
8. When traveling, bring grain that has been washed and dry-roasted, along with sea salt and a wide mouth thermos. Just obtain boiling water and let your grains "cook" in the thermos while you travel.
9. Pan or dry-roasting grains makes them cook more quickly, but

does not make them more yang.

10. Grain can be cooked in the morning to be served in the evening.

11. Leftover breakfast grains or other grains can be mashed or blended and used to thicken salad dressings, puddings, soups, or sauces, especially for those people who avoid flour products.

Cooking Beans

1. Prepare enough for more than one meal, leaving the extra amount undercooked.

2. Plan ahead how you will be using them: plain, with vegetables, with grains, with sea vegetables, in soups, in salads, in desserts, sandwich spreads, or as snacks.

3. Soak overnight and cook early in the morning, turn off before leaving, and continue cooking when you return, in a manner similar to adding vegetables and seasonings.

4. To help beans cook more quickly, soak overnight, cook in the smallest, heavy pot you can, use a 1- or 2-inch-square of kombu under the beans while cooking, and cook with just enough water to cover, adding water as needed. Do not stir while cooking, add seasoning after beans are soft, and continue cooking, 10 to 20 minutes for sea salt; 5 minutes for miso or shoyu.

5. Pressure cooking is a quick way to cook beans, but when pressure is used for other products, it becomes too yang to prepare beans that way also. Save pressure cooking beans for when they are cooked with a whole grain, possibly for chickpeas or soybeans, or once in a great while (during cold weather) for other types of beans.

6. Use tempeh and tofu on days when whole beans are not cooked.

7. Use quick cooking beans like red lentils and split peas.

8. Skip beans once in a while; other times use more than one bean and/or bean product in the same meal, especially when you need to use up leftovers.

9. Beans are not needed when fish is served.

Cooking Vegetables

1. Plan meals ahead so you only have to shop once a week.
2. If you are cooking for one or two people, try to shop with a friend (or take turns shopping) and share the vegetables. This will help you eliminate having to eat the same vegetables day after day, trying to use them up or have them go bad because they are only in large bunches or large heads.
3. Extra pieces of vegetables can be used for pickles.
4. Vegetable dishes that take longer to cook can be used for two days, keeping in mind that reheating them makes them more yang. Therefore, on the second day, remove the dish from the refrigerator early and let warm up to room temperature and then serve.
5. Keep brine and shoyu pickles fermenting on your counter. Every day take some out to use and add a few pieces of raw vegetables as you cut them up for cooking for dinner.
6. If you will be returning home late to prepare dinner, wash, slice, and bag up your vegetables in the morning before you leave, keeping in mind that they will have less energy.
7. Fine creative ways to use leftover vegetables. Steamed, quick boiled, pressed, or raw, they can be used in salad, soup, stir fries, or just mixed into a grain or breakfast cereal.
8. Blended or mashed, vegetables can be used for spreads, soups, dressings, or sauces.

Odds and Ends

1. Prepare dry condiments once a week. Plan ahead for your day off (ha, ha!), make enough for one week, and plan to make a fresh condiment once or twice a week.
2. Check macrobiotic directories and put notices up in health food stores, vegetable markets, food coops, new age stores and book stores to locate other macrobiotic friends to start support groups, pot luck dinners, or cooking clubs where participants take turns cooking meals in their own homes and the others just stop by and pick up their meals on the nights they do not cook.
3. Make use of meals to go services.

4. Frequent and get to know a local restaurant, requesting brown rice, steamed vegetables, and anything else simple to cook which they could incorporate into their menu.

5. When traveling, check a macro directory and write ahead to people and businesses in the area you will be passing through and arrange to have meals waiting (at modest cost) or inquire where you can go to purchase meals or products to cook. (One Peaceful World Press publishes a regular, up-to-date directory of macrobiotic resources across the country and around the world.)

6. When traveling, make use of macrobiotic mail order companies and have food and/or cooking equipment sent directly to your destination. Or you may send it ahead by UPS to anywhere in the continental U.S. within 5 days.

7. Creating soups, stews, salads, etc. out of leftovers saves a great deal of time. Plan your meals, foresee cooking extra food as needed, and anticipate how you will use leftovers.

8. Prepare one dish meals occasionally.

9. Sing a happy song every day.

Week 1

Day 1

Breakfast

Miso Soup
Oatmeal with Raisins
Blanched Bok Choy

MISO SOUP

4 cups water
2-inch piece dried wakame
3- to 4-inch piece of daikon
1 or 2 leaves Chinese cabbage
1 $1/2$ tsp. well aged barley miso
sliced scallions

- Rinse wakame, soak for 3 to 5 minutes, discard soaking water, and cut into small pieces. Place wakame and water in a pot and bring to a boil.
- Wash vegetables and slice very fine. Add to boiling water, return to a boil, lower flame, and simmer for 3 minutes.
- Dilute miso in a little water, add to soup, and simmer on a very low flame for 3 minutes. Garnish individual bowls with scallions.

OATMEAL WITH RAISINS

1¼ cups rolled oats
pinch of sea salt
3 to 4 cups water
¼ cup raisins

• In cold weather, toast oats in a heavy, dry skillet on a medium flame for 5 minutes.
• Place oats, salt, and water in a thick pot, cover, and bring to a boil on a high flame, stirring occasionally. Lower flame and simmer for 30 minutes using a flame deflector and stirring occasionally (less time is needed if oats are toasted).
• Stir in raisins for the last 5 minutes of cooking time.

BLANCHED BOK CHOY

1 or 2 whole bok choy leaves per person
2 inches of water

• Boil water in a thin pot.
• Wash leaves and slice into 2-inch-long pieces
• Place leaves a few at a time in water, do not crowd, return to a boil, and scoop out leaves.
• Drain well in a strainer and place on a platter to cool so leaves do not continue to cook.
• Continue until all the leaves are done (water can be saved to use in broth for lunch).

Lunch

Somen Noodles
Kombu Broth (Dashi)
Deep Fried Tofu
Watercress

SOMEN NOODLES

1 lb. whole wheat somen (thin) noodles (use unsalted regular whole wheat noodles for young children)

- Bring a large pot of water to a boil, add noodles, and stir well.
- When water returns to a boil, add a little cold water and let return to a boil. Stir often and repeat until noodles are done (somen cooks in under 10 minutes).
- Drain noodles and rinse with cold water to remove some of the remaining salt. Noodles can be rinsed with warm water before serving if stuck together.

KOMBU BROTH (DASHI)

1 6-inch piece of kombu, wiped clean, soaked for a few minutes, and then cut several times in each side
4 to 5 cups of water
shoyu (about 2 Tbs.)
strips of toasted nori sea vegetable.
sliced scallions

- Place kombu and water in a pot, cover, and bring to a boil. Remove kombu and save to cook with beans for dinner. Season water with shoyu. You may want to use two pots, the first with reduced seasoning for young children or those restricting their salt intake and the second with more shoyu for adults and active older children.
- Simmer 5 minutes.

DEEP FRIED TOFU

$1/2$ to 1 lb. tofu
2 inches deep-frying oil (toasted sesame or safflower)
$1/2$ cup whole wheat pastry flour
shoyu
pinch of sea salt

- Gently squeeze liquid out of tofu and slice into 4 pieces for each $1/2$ lb.
- Place slices on a paper towel on a plate. Cover with another paper towel and another plate. Place a light weight on top (e.g., a jar of water) and let sit while oil heats.
- Put 2 inches of oil in a cast-iron or heavy pot. Heat but do not let it smoke.
- Mix flour and salt, cover both sides of each piece of tofu with flour, and place a few slices at a time in the oil. Cook until lightly golden on both sides.
- Drain well on paper towels and sprinkle with a few drops of shoyu.
- If avoiding flour and oil, cut up tofu and simmer in broth.
- In individual bowls place some noodles, cover with broth, add watercress and tofu, and garnish with scallions and nori.

WATERCRESS

1 bunch watercress

- Pull leaves apart, wash carefully, and leave whole or cut into 1-inch-long pieces.
- Blanch watercress, drain, and let cool off.

Dinner

Pressure-Cooked Short Grain Brown Rice
Millet with Squash or Corn
Kidney Beans with Onions
Nishime Style Vegetables
Sautéed Kale
Pumpkin Seed Condiment

PRESSURE-COOKED SHORT GRAIN BROWN RICE

In hot weather, try long-grain brown rice.

3 cups short grain brown rice
$3^3/_4$ to 4 cups water
2 pinches of sea salt

- Spread rice on a plate and pick through to remove any stones or shells.
- Gently rinse rice in a bowl with cool water a few times, pouring water off through a strainer until water is clear.
- Place rice and water in a pressure cooker without the lid. Put on a low flame for 10 minutes. Add salt and secure lid. Turn flame to high and bring pressure up.
- When full pressure is up (gauge is actively hissing and spinning on most cookers) lower flame, place a flame deflector under pot, and cook for 50 minutes.
- Remove from heat and let pressure drop. Gently scoop rice into a wooden bowl and cover with a bamboo mat.

MILLET WITH SQUASH OR CORN

$1^1/_2$ cups millet
3 cups water
$1/_2$ cup diced winter squash (butternut, buttercup, or Hokaido) or corn kernels cut off the cob
$1/_2$ to 1 tsp. shoyu

- Bring water to a boil in a covered pot.
- Wash millet the same way rice was washed, using a fine mesh strainer to drain it.
- In cool weather, drain millet well and roast in a dry, hot skillet for 5 minutes or until golden.
- Add millet, squash, and shoyu to the pot, return to a boil, lower heat, and simmer 25 minutes (20 minutes if roasted). If using corn, add it during the last 5 minutes of cooking time.

KIDNEY BEANS AND ONIONS

1 cup dried beans (increase amount for more leftovers)
1 cup onions, sliced
3 to 4 cups of water
1 tsp. sweet miso
1-inch-square piece of kombu or kombu from lunch broth

- Pick through beans and wash. Add water and soak overnight or at least 4 hours (Beans can be cooked early in the morning, started any time during the day or started early, turned off, and finished later).
- Place kombu in a heavy pot, put beans on top, and add just enough of the soaking water to cover the beans. Cover pot and bring to a boil, lower the flame, and simmer for at least 2 hours longer for easier digestion.
- Check beans often, adding more water as needed to keep water level just to the top of the beans. Do not stir.
- When beans soften, place onions on top, cover the pot, and simmer until onions are soft.
- Place miso on top of onions, cover, and simmer 3 to 5 minutes. Do not add more water after adding miso. Gently stir, cover, turn off the flame, and let sit for 5 minutes before serving.
- For variety, add a little brown rice vinegar and/or a pinch of dry mustard when miso is added.

NISHIME STYLE VEGETABLES

In warmer weather, cut vegetables smaller and cook less time.

1 4- to 6-inch strip of kombu, wiped clean and soaked for 5 minutes
1 carrot, 1 turnip, 2 shiitakes rinsed and soaked 15 minutes or until soft
1 2-inch piece of fresh lotus root or 4 small pieces of dried lotus soaked for a half hour
shoyu

- Slice kombu into $1/4$-inch strips and place on bottom of a heavy pot.

- Wash carrots and cut into 1½-inch slices.
- Wash turnip and cut into 1 to 1½-inch cubes or chunks.
- Cut tip off shiitake stems and discard, and slice mushrooms and stems.
- Slice lotus into thin rounds.
- Place vegetables in the pot, giving each one its own space (they can be touching to fit all into the pot). Add water to just cover the kombu and slightly up the sides of the vegetables.
- Optional: For a sweeter but more yang (contracting) dish, sprinkle with a little sea salt.
- Cover pot and bring to a boil, lower flame, and simmer for 20 minutes or until vegetables are soft. Sprinkle with a little shoyu and simmer 5 more minutes.
- Gently scoop out vegetables into a serving dish and save remaining liquid to use with leftovers.

SAUTEED KALE

1 small bunch of kale
2 tsp. sesame or corn oil
shoyu

- Cut kale leaves from hard center stem and wash carefully. Discard center stem and cut stems from leaves.
- Slice stems into 2-inch-long pieces on a diagonal, and slice leaves into 2-inch squares, keeping leaves and stems separate.
- Heat a skillet, add oil, and when hot add stems and sauté on a medium flame for a few minutes. Add leaves and sauté for a few more minutes. Add 1 Tbs. of water, sprinkle with a few drops of shoyu, cover, lower flame, and simmer for 3 minutes. Serve warm.

PUMPKIN SEED CONDIMENT

½ cup raw pumpkin seeds (not in shells)
1 tsp. dried shiso powder

- Wash pumpkin seeds and drain well in a strainer.

- Heat a heavy stainless steel skillet, add seeds, and stir for about 10 minutes or until seeds are dry and lightly browned on a medium-low flame. They should crack open easily when bent and be dry inside.
- Grind seeds in a suribachi until almost totally crushed then add shiso, and grind until well mixed.
- When cool, store in an airtight container, and serve over grains, noodles, or vegetables.

Day 2

Breakfast

Soft Millet
Dulse Miso Soup
Steamed Broccoli

SOFT MILLET

leftover millet
$1/2$ to $3/4$ cups water for each cup of millet

- Put water and millet in a heavy pot and/or use a flame deflector and bring to a boil. Lower flame and simmer about 15 minutes, stirring occasionally until all water is absorbed. Use extra water and make a softer cereal if your condition tends to be tight or dry (too yang).

DULSE MISO SOUP

1 onion, sliced thin
$1/2$ cup cauliflower, sliced into small pieces
2 tsp. dry dulse
4 cups of water

1 1/2 tsp. brown rice miso
sliced parsley

• Rinse dulse and cut up fine.
• Boil water with vegetables, add dulse, lower flame, and simmer for 5 minutes.
• Dilute miso in a little water and stir into soup, and simmer with the lid off for 3 minutes.
• Garnish with parsley.

STEAMED BROCCOLI

Steaming is a slightly more yang method of cooking than quick boiling and is used more often in cooler weather.

1/2 head of broccoli

• Wash broccoli and cut off any hard ends and tough skin on stems. Slice stems into small rounds or strips and cut flowers into 2- to 3-inch-sized pieces with a slit in any thick stems attached to flowers.
• Put a little water in a thin pan, place a steamer basket inside, and bring to a boil. Put in some pieces of broccoli, cover, and steam until soft but still bright green and a little crisp. Do not overcrowd the basket or the pieces will not cook evenly. Cook flowers separately from stems. Place on a serving platter as each piece is done to cool so they will not continue to cook.

Lunch

Fried Rice
Nishime With Kuzu Sauce
Boiled Mustard Greens

FRIED RICE

1 1/2 cups leftover rice
1/2 leek, thinly sliced
1/2 cup fresh mushrooms, sliced (optional)
1/2 cup edible pea pods, whole or sliced
1 Tbs. corn, sesame, or olive oil
few drops of shoyu
1 scallion, finely sliced

- Heat a heavy skillet and add oil. Add leeks and mushrooms and stir on a medium flame for 10 minutes.
- Add 1/4 cup of water, place rice on top, and sprinkle with shoyu and scallions. Cover and simmer on a low flame for 5 minutes. Stir well and serve.

NISHIME WITH KUZU SAUCE

leftover nishime
1 cup leftover cooking water or fresh water with a little shoyu added
1 heaping tsp. kuzu

- In a small pan, mix kuzu into cold liquid, bring to a boil stirring constantly, lower flame, and simmer for 5 minutes.
- Stir sauce into vegetables and serve.

BOILED MUSTARD GREENS

1 bunch mustard greens
lemon or brown rice vinegar

- Wash leaves carefully to remove all hidden sand. Cut into 1- or 2-inch-long pieces.
- Boil 2 inches of water and cook as in directions for blanched bok choy, except let mustard greens cook slightly longer before removing.
- Sprinkle with lemon juice or brown rice vinegar.

Dinner

Medium Grain Rice with Whole Oats
Kidney Bean Soup
Kinpira
Arame Vegetables
Collard Greens
Gomashio

MEDIUM GRAIN RICE WITH WHOLE OATS

The cool temperatures of spring and fall are ideal for medium-grain rice, less energetic (warming) than short-grain and more strengthening than long-grain.

$2^3/_4$ cups medium grain brown rice
$1/_4$ cup whole oats
$4^1/_2$ cups water
2 pinches sea salt

• Wash grains, add water, and soak 4 to 6 hours.
• Place in a pressure cooker with salt, secure lid, and bring pressure up on a high flame. When pressure is up, lower flame, and cook on a flame deflector for 55 minutes.
• Use a little less water for a more dry grain dish.
• Gently scoop into a serving bowl when pressure is down.

KIDNEY BEAN SOUP

leftover kidney beans
$1/2$ cup celery, sliced
$1/2$ cup carrots, sliced
$1/4$ cup parsnips, sliced
$1/4$ cup uncooked elbow or small shell noodles
2 tsp. umeboshi vinegar
chives or parsley for garnish, sliced
5 cups of water

- In a tall soup pot, layer vegetables starting with celery, then parsnips, then carrots. In warmer weather, substitute string beans for parsnips and cut vegetables smaller. Simmer for 10 minutes. Place beans on top and gently pour water down the side, trying not to disturb the layering.
- Bring to a boil on a medium flame, add noodles, and return to a boil. Add vinegar and simmer for 15 minutes. Stir well before serving and garnish.

KINPIRA

1 cup carrots, finely sliced into matchsticks
$1/2$ cup burdock root, finely sliced or shaved
$1/4$ to $1/2$ cup lotus root, cut into thin rounds and then cut in half
toasted sesame oil
several drops of shoyu
juice from 1 tsp. fresh ginger, grated

- Heat a skillet, brush with oil, and when hot add burdock. Sauté for 5 minutes on a medium flame. Layer carrots and then lotus on top of burdock.
- Add just enough water to cover the burdock. Cover skillet and simmer for 20 minutes.
- Add shoyu, cover, and simmer until water has evaporated.
- Add a few drops of ginger juice and stir well.

ARAME WITH VEGETABLES

$1/4$ cup dried arame sea vegetable
1 medium-sized onion, sliced into half-moons
$1/2$ winter or summer squash, cut into slices
$1/2$ tsp. sesame oil
$1/2$ tsp. shoyu

- Rinse arame and let sit in a strainer while a skillet is heated.
- Add oil, when hot add arame, and sauté on a medium flame for a few minutes.
- Place onions on top of arame and then squash on top of the onions. Add enough water to just cover the arame, cover the skillet, and simmer on a low flame for 15 minutes.
- Sprinkle with shoyu, cover, and simmer for 5 more minutes. Stir well before serving.

COLLARD GREENS

1 small bunch of collards

- Pull individual leaves and stems off the center stem, discard the thick center stem, and wash.
- Cut stems from leaves and slice the stems into $1/4$-inch-long pieces on a diagonal for easier chewing or 2 inches long for a sweeter taste. Slice leaves into 2-inch squares and keep them separate from the stems.
- Proceed as in boiled bok choy (*see Breakfast Day 1*), except let the collards cook for about $1 1/2$ minutes before removing, cooking stems separately from leaves because they take slightly longer.

GOMASHIO
(Sesame Seed and Sea Salt Condiment)

18 parts brown or black sesame seeds (6 Tbs.)
1 part sea salt (1 tsp.)

• Pick through sesame seeds to remove any sticks, shells, or dirt; wash in a bowl; and drain through a fine mesh strainer.
• Heat a heavy stainless steel skillet, and dry-roast the sea salt on a medium-high flame, stirring constantly until the color turns slightly gray.
• Put the salt in a suribachi and grind into a very fine powder.
• Roast the seeds in the same pot on a medium flame. Stir gently. The seeds are done when they crush easily between the thumb and index finger, after 5 to 10 minutes cooking time. Shake skillet occasionally while cooking.
• Add the seeds while they are still hot to the ground salt. Gently crush the seeds in a circular motion, using the grooved sides of the bowl to do the grinding. Grind until all the seeds are crushed and the salt is thoroughly mixed in.
• After the gomashio cools, store in an airtight container,
• Make enough to last for a week or less for freshness.
• For a higher iron content use black seeds.
• Make more than one condiment, adjusting the salt to fit the needs of all those you cook for. Also you may wish to make some gomashio with black seeds and some with brown seeds.
• Serve 1 tsp. or less a day over grains or vegetables.
• Roast extra seeds, cool and store in a jar to use in a future dish.

Day 3

Breakfast

Soft Sweet Rice and Oats with Dry Fruit
Steamed Greens
Bancha Tea

SOFT SWEET RICE AND OATS WITH DRY FRUIT

½ cup whole oats
½ cup sweet brown rice
4 cups of water
½ cup dried fruit (apples, pears, etc.)
1 pinch of sea salt

• Rinse and soak dried fruit until soft (saving the liquid) and dice the fruit.
• Wash grains and soak 4 to 8 hours. Place grains, salt, and soaking water in a pressure cooker and cook under full pressure for one hour.
• When pressure is down, remove lid and stir well. Add more water if softer cereal is desired and cook a little longer.
• Add fruit and soaking water, stir well, and simmer for 5 minutes or until fruit is soft.
• In spring, try fresh berries instead of dry fruit.

STEAMED GREENS

kale, collards, watercress, leeks, mustard, Chinese cabbage, bok choy, etc.

- Wash and slice any one of the above or several (a good time to use up small bits of unused veggies)
- Place vegetables in $1/2$-inch of boiling water or in a stainless steel or bamboo steamer basket above a little boiling water.
- Do not crowd vegetables or cook thick stems with thin leaves.
- Cover and steam for 1 to 3 minutes, depending on texture of vegetables and size cut.
- Transfer leaves while still bright green to a serving dish to prevent overcooking.

BANCHA TEA

1 Tbs. bancha twigs
2 cups water

- Boil water, add twigs, lower flame, and simmer for 5 minutes. Strain out twigs and save as each cup is poured. Put twigs back in pot, add more water when tea is used up, and make another pot from same twigs, reheating as needed. Bancha tea generally tastes best prepared in a glass pot.
- Drink a small cup after meals or when thirsty.

Lunch

Tofu Sandwiches
Sandwich Spread
Cucumber Pickles

TOFU SANDWICHES

4 sandwich-size slices of tofu
corn oil
sourdough bread, sliced
shoyu, a few drops
sandwich fixings: lettuce, sprouts, sliced red onion, sauerkraut,

sliced pickles
- In a hot oiled skillet, fry tofu a few minutes on each side sprinkled with shoyu and drain on a paper towel.
- Optional: Sandwich can be made crisp by frying the whole sandwich for a few minutes on each side in a lightly oiled hot skillet before adding raw fixings.

SANDWICH SPREAD

1 Tbs. tahini
1 tsp. umeboshi paste
1 scallion, sliced
2 tsp. brown rice vinegar

- In a small pan, mix tahini, umeboshi, and vinegar; heat on a low flame for a few minutes; and cool and spread on bread. Add a slice of tofu and choice of fixings.

CUCUMBER PICKLES

Pickling cucumbers are at their best in spring and summer.

6 to 8 small pickling cucumbers
5 cups water
2 Tbs. sea salt
few sprigs of fresh dill weed or 2 tsp. dry dill weed or seed
1 clove of garlic, crushed or sliced (optional)
cheesecloth and a rubber band
1 wide-mouth gallon jar or 4 1-qt. jars

- Bring water and salt to a boil, lower flame, and simmer for 5 minutes or until salt has dissolved. Let water cool.
- Carefully wash cucumbers and cut off any decaying parts. Dry cucumbers completely with a towel.
- Place cucumbers, dill, garlic, and salt water in clean, dry jars.
- To keep cucumbers under the surface of the water, place a cabbage leaf on top of them, held in place by the sides of the jar.

- Cover each jar with a piece of cheesecloth and secure with a rubber band.
- Place jars away from sunlight but where air can circulate.
- Leave for a few days, up to a week, until cucumbers become light green and no longer have a salty taste.
- In a hot climate, place jar directly in refrigerator to pickle.
- Refrigerate and slice as needed.
- Liquid can be used to make new pickles if not moldy. Strained liquid can be used in cooking or salad dressings.

Dinner

Boiled Long Grain Rice
Chickpeas and Fu
Vegetable Stew
Pressed Salad
Bok Choy Stir Fry
Shoyu and Vinegar Pickles

BOILED LONG GRAIN RICE

Boiled grain is less strengthening and is usually enjoyed more often in the summer.

2 cups long grain brown rice
2 pinches sea salt
4 cups water

- Wash rice. Boil water and salt, add rice, cover, lower flame, and simmer $1\frac{1}{4}$ hours.

CHICKPEAS AND FU

1 cup dried chickpeas
2 rings or 2 flat sheets of whole wheat fu
3 cups water
2-inch-square piece of kombu
1 pinch sea salt
1 tsp. chickpea or sweet light miso

- Pick through and wash chickpeas, add water, and soak for 4 to 8 hours.
- Place kombu in a pressure cooker and place chickpeas and soaking water on top.
- Cook under pressure for a half hour if soaked for 6 to 8 hrs, and for 45 minutes if soaked for less time.
- Remove from heat, let pressure come down naturally, and remove lid.
- Soak fu until soft, and cut each ring into 6 pieces, or 8 slices if using flat fu.
- Add fu and miso to pot, cover but do not secure pressure lid, and simmer on a low flame for 5 minutes.
- Stir well, scoop out chickpeas and fu, and save any remaining liquid.

VEGETABLE STEW

1 cup of root vegetables cut into small chunks (e.g., onion, carrot, turnip, rutabaga, lotus, daikon, or burdock)
1 cup of one, or a combination, of the following vegetables: cabbage, Chinese cabbage, winter squash, summer squash, sweet corn, snap peas, snow peas, or scallions, cut into 2-inch-long pieces
1 4-inch strip of kombu, wiped clean of excess salt and soaked in 2 cups of water
2 to 3 scallions or a few sprigs of watercress
shoyu, a few drops

- Cut kombu into small pieces; place kombu, soaking water and root

vegetables in a pot; and bring to a boil. Lower flame and simmer for about 15 minutes. Add other vegetables and shoyu, and simmer 5 more minutes or until soft.
• Add thin cut scallions or watercress and cook for 1 minute or less.
• A small amount of ginger juice can be added at the end of the cooking time.
• Gently scoop out vegetables and save liquid to use to reheat leftovers or thicken with kuzu and pour over vegetables.

PRESSED SALAD

2 cups nappa cabbage, thinly sliced
1 cucumber, thinly sliced and peeled if waxed or oiled
3 red radishes, grated on a cheese grater
1 $1/2$ tsp. sea salt
brown rice vinegar or umeboshi vinegar

• Mix salt into vegetables, gently rubbing it in. Place vegetables in a vegetable press and apply pressure. Let sit for 10 minutes. If no water has come out of the vegetables, the vegetables have not been cut finely enough or not enough salt has been added.
• Add a little more salt and press a little longer, until you can see water in the press.
• Remove vegetables and rinse well to remove all salt.
• Place in a serving bowl and sprinkle with vinegar.

BOK CHOY STIR FRY

1 bunch bok choy
1 tsp. olive oil
shoyu

• Separate leaves and wash. Slice green and white parts of the leaves into thin diagonal slices.
• Heat a wok or frying pan and add oil. When oil is hot, add bok choy and sprinkle with a little shoyu. Sauté, stirring constantly on a high flame for about 3 minutes.

- Place on a serving platter and serve while still warm.
- Optional: Sauté with water instead of oil if choosing to restrict your oil intake.

SHOYU-VINEGAR PICKLES

$1/2$ cup of turnip, daikon, or onion, thinly sliced
$1/4$ cup shoyu
$1/4$ cup water
1 Tbs. brown rice vinegar

- Mix shoyu and water in a small saucepan. Heat for a few minutes on a low flame and let cool.
- Place all ingredients in a small crock, bowl, or jar. Cover with a piece of cheesecloth and put a rubber band around the top to hold the cloth in place.
- Let sit for a few days before using, and rinse or soak pieces before giving to children. Store in a refrigerator after one week. Liquid can be used again for one or two more batches, adding a little more shoyu each time.

Day 4

Breakfast

Whole Barley with Sweet Rice
Miso Soup with Fried Mochi
Broccoli Rabi

WHOLE BARLEY WITH SWEET RICE

$1/2$ cup whole barley
$1/2$ cup sweet rice
4 cups water
1-inch square of kombu

2 small onions, cut into quarters

• Wash and soak grains together 4 to 8 hours.
• Put kombu in a pressure cooker, and making sure the kombu stays on the bottom of the pot, add grain and soaking water. Cook under pressure for $1\frac{1}{2}$ hours or simmer for 2 to 3 hours in a heavy pot over a flame deflector, adding water as needed. (This dish may be cooked during the evening, reheated, and served the next morning.)
• Add onions after pressure comes down, stir well, and simmer 10 minutes or onions are soft.
• Optional: In warm weather, boiled cereal would be less warming. Increase water to 6 cups.

MISO SOUP WITH FRIED MOCHI

2-inch piece of wakame rinsed, soaked, and cut up into small pieces
2 onions, sliced into thin half-moons
4 cups of water
scallions or chives, sliced for garnish
3 tsp. barley miso
4 2-inch squares of mochi
oil for deep-frying (two inches)

• Heat oil, drop in mochi, and cook until lightly browned on all sides. Drain well. Squeeze some oil out with paper towels.
• Place wakame, onions, and then the mochi in a soup pot. Add water, cover, and bring to a boil.
• Lower flame and simmer for 3 minutes. Dilute miso in a little water, stir into soup, and simmer for 3 minutes. Serve with garnish.

BROCCOLI RABI

1 small bunch of greens
lemon juice

• Wash greens, cut up into $\frac{1}{2}$ to 1-inch pieces, steam, and sprinkle with lemon juice.

Lunch

Pasta Salad
Pasta Sauce
Sweet Vegetable Drink

PASTA SALAD

3/4 lb. shell or spiral pasta
leftover pressed salad
olive oil

- Cook pasta until done but still firm. Put a few drops of olive oil in the cooking water to keep pasta from sticking together and a few grains of sea salt. Drain well and cool.
- Mix pressed vegetables with pasta.

PASTA SAUCE

3 Tbs. sesame tahini
1 Tbs. white or chickpea miso
1/2 cup water
1 tsp. olive oil
1 Tbs. fresh lemon juice
1/4 tsp. basil (fresh is best)
1/4 tsp. powdered shiso leaf
1/4 cup chives or scallions, finely sliced

- Blend tahini, miso, water, and olive oil. Heat a few minutes on a low flame and cool. Stir in basil, shiso, and chives. Mix into salad and chill.

SWEET VEGETABLE DRINK

1/4 cup onion, finely diced
1/4 cup carrot, finely cut or grated (catch all the juice)

¼ cup sweet winter squash, finely cut
¼ cup head or Chinese cabbage, finely cut
4 cups of water

• Boil water, add vegetables, bring back to a boil, lower flame, and simmer for 20 minutes. Scoop out vegetables, and squeeze all the liquid out into drink. Save the vegetables.
• Drink the broth hot or room temperature.

Heat leftover vegetable stew for lunch

Dinner

Broccoli Soup
Steamed Rice
Chickpea Sauce
Daikon Nishime and Greens
Baked Squash and Onions

BROCCOLI SOUP

1 head of broccoli
5 cups of water
2 inch piece of wakame
2 tsp. sweet miso
¼ cup toasted brown sesame seeds
sliced scallions for garnish

• Wash broccoli, cut stems into thin rounds or strips, and slice heads into very small flowerettes.
• Rinse, soak, and cut up wakame. Bring water and wakame to a boil. Add stems, return to a boil, and add flowers.
• Grind seeds in a suribachi until all are crushed, and add to soup.
• Dilute miso in a little soup water, stir into soup, and simmer for 3 minutes.
• Serve with garnish.

STEAMED RICE

2 to 3 cups leftover boiled rice
1 cup corn, cut off the cob

• Mix corn into rice. Steam in a steamer basket for 5 minutes or until rice is hot and corn is cooked.

CHICKPEA SAUCE

1 cup leftover chickpeas
1 tsp. tahini
2 Tbs. grated onion
1 tsp. umeboshi paste
2 tsp. brown rice vinegar
1 Tbs. minced parsley

• Mix tahini, onion, paste, and vinegar; heat for a few minutes on a low flame; and let cool.
• Purée the chickpeas in a hand food mill or food processor, adding some of the cooking water if too thick and the cooked ingredients.
• Serve over rice or use as a dip or spread on rice cakes or chips.

DAIKON NISHIME WITH GREENS

1 daikon
4-inch strip of kombu, wiped clean and soaked for a few minutes
daikon greens (or turnip greens)

• Cut kombu into 1-inch-square pieces and place in a heavy dry pot.
• Wash daikon, cut into 2-inch-long pieces, and place in pot.
• Wash greens and slice into $1/2$- to 1-inch-long pieces.
• Add 1 to 2 inches of water, cover, and bring to a boil. Lower flame and simmer for 15 to 20 minutes (until daikon is soft). (In warm weather, cut kombu and daikon smaller and cook with less time).
• Place greens on top of daikon, cover, and simmer for 3 more min-

utes.
- Mix greens, roots, and kombu in a serving dish.

BAKED SQUASH AND ONIONS

1 acorn or small butternut squash
2 onions, cut in half
corn oil
sea salt
shoyu

- Preheat oven to 350 degrees.
- Wash squash, and cut off hard ends and any hard spots or bumps on the skin.
- Cut open and scoop out the seeds. Cut acorn into 4 pieces, and cut the butternut squash into large chunks.
- Brush pieces of squash with oil, sprinkle with sea salt, and place in a baking dish with onions. (You may use a little water instead of oil and omit salt, if desired.)
- Cover and bake for 25 minutes or just until squash and onions are soft. Sprinkle with shoyu. Bake for a few more minutes and serve warm.
- For young children and people with a yang condition, steam squash and onions instead of baking. Use yellow summer squash when in season.

Day 5

Breakfast

Sourdough Pancakes
Lemon Rice Syrup Sauce
Barley Tea
Quick Onion Pickles
Heat Leftover Broccoli Soup

SOURDOUGH PANCAKES

3/4 cup whole wheat pastry flour
3/4 cup whole wheat bread flour
2 Tbs. corn oil
extra oil for the pan
1/8 tsp. sea salt
1 cup cooked soft rice or breakfast cereal (puréed grain)
2 cups soured seitan or noodle water (water saved from homemade seitan or cooking water from noodles)
blueberries (optional)

- Combine all ingredients (except blueberries), and let sit overnight in a warm place covered with a mat or towel.
- Heat a cast-iron or heavy frying pan and brush with oil.
- Stir berries into batter.
- Pour 1/4 cup of batter for each pancake and cook on a medium flame for a few minutes on each side, until golden.
- Keep warm until ready to serve or reheat in a steamer basket.

LEMON RICE SYRUP SAUCE

1/2 cup brown rice syrup
pinch of sea salt
4 tsp. arrowroot flour
1/2 cup water or apple juice
2 tsp. fresh squeezed lemon juice

- Bring water, salt, and rice syrup to a boil. Dissolve the arrowroot in a little liquid and stir in. Stir until mixture returns to a boil, lower the flame, and simmer for 5 minutes, adding the lemon juice for the last few minutes.
- Serve warm over the pancakes.

BARLEY TEA

Barley tea is commonly sold in the natural foods store as "Mugi Cha." For a relaxing, more yin barley tea, use whole grain barley and dry roast it on top of the stove for at least 10 minutes or until it is as dark as desired.

- Boil 2 cups of water, lower flame, and add 2 or 3 tsp. of barley tea. With the lid off, simmer for 5 minutes.
- Use more or less tea to taste. Barley can be reused for a second pot of weaker tea.

QUICK ONION PICKLE

1/2 onion, sliced into fine half moons or rounds
shoyu

- Boil 2 inches of water in a small pot, drop in a few pieces of onion at a time, and scoop out almost immediately. Drain well and let cool.
- Place onions in a bowl and cover with shoyu or 1/2 shoyu and 1/2 water.
- Let sit for at least one half hour before serving. Rinse or soak if too salty.

Lunch

Fried Couscous
Leftover Veggies

FRIED COUSCOUS

1 cup yellow couscous
2 1/2 cups water
1 small onion, thinly sliced

¼ cup carrot, finely sliced or grated or corn kernels in summer
¼ cup fresh peas and/or mung bean sprouts
1 Tbs. sesame or corn oil
½ to 1 tsp. shoyu

• Boil water with a pinch of sea salt, add couscous, return to a boil, and turn off flame. Let pot sit covered for a few minutes, until all water is absorbed. For whole wheat couscous, use 3 cups of water and simmer for 10 minutes.
• Heat a skillet and add oil. Sauté onions for a few minutes, and add carrots, sautéing for a few more minutes.
• Stir in couscous, shoyu, peas, and sprouts. Sprinkle with a little water, cover, and simmer on a low flame for 3 minutes.

LEFTOVER VEGGIES

leftover nishime and squash and onions
¼ cup mochi, grated
¼ cup parsley, minced

• Heat leftovers in a steamer basket.
• Mix mochi into ¾ cup of water or any vegetable cooking water you have saved. Heat mixture on a medium flame, stirring constantly until mochi is melted.
• Place vegetables in a bowl, pour mochi sauce on top, sprinkle with parsley, and serve.

Dinner

Creamed Cauliflower Soup
Millet with Onions
Aduki-Kombu-Squash
Steamed Broccoli
Pressed Cucumbers
Scallion-Miso Condiment

CREAMED CAULIFLOWER SOUP

1 head cauliflower
4 to 5 cups water
1 3-inch strip of kombu
2 tsp. natto miso or sweet rice miso (the word "natto" means condiment; this condiment that contains kombu and ginger and can be used as a seasoning in soups and sauces)
sliced parsley for garnish

- Wash and cut cauliflower and soft parts of stem and core into small pieces or slices.
- Steam pieces over 2 cups of boiling water and kombu. Remove kombu and save water.
- Purée cauliflower and stir into water saved from steaming. Add more water for desired consistency and simmer on a medium flame for 10 minutes. Stir in miso and simmer for 5 more minutes. Serve warm with garnish.

MILLET WITH ONIONS

2 cups dried millet
1 pinch sea salt
3 cups water
2 onion, diced
2 tsp. corn or sesame oil
1 tsp. shoyu

- Bring water and salt to a boil. Wash, drain, and lightly toast millet in a dry skillet until just a little golden (about 5 minutes).
- Sauté onions in oil for 5 minutes.
- Add millet and onions to water, return to a boil, lower flame, and simmer for 20 minutes. Add shoyu and simmer for 5 more minutes.

ADUKI-KOMBU-SQUASH

1 cup dried aduki (adzuki) beans
2 2-inch squares of kombu
1 cup winter squash, cut into large chunks
2 pinches sea salt

- Clean beans and soak for a few hours with enough water to cover, plus one inch of water.
- Place beans with soaking water in a heavy pot, and place kombu on top. Cover and bring to a boil, lower flame, and simmer until beans are almost done, about one hour. Add a little water as needed to keep water level just to the top of the beans.
- Lift kombu off beans (it will have fallen apart so scoop off as much as possible), and place it in another heavy pot. Place squash on top of kombu and gently pour beans and remaining water on top. Cover and simmer until beans and squash are soft, adding a little more water if beans are dry.
- Sprinkle salt over beans and simmer for 15 minutes. Stir well but gently, as this dish is not stirred during cooking.

STEAMED BROCCOLI

1 head broccoli

- Wash broccoli and cut off hard or decaying ends of stems. Peel or cut off any tough skins on stems. Slice stems into thin rounds or strips. Cut heads into edible size pieces.
- Cook pieces in a steamer a little at a time. Do not crowd or they will not cook evenly.
- Broccoli should be soft enough to chew easily but bright green in color and still a little crisp.
- Place cooked pieces on a platter and let cool briefly so they do not continue to cook after taken from steamer.

PRESSED CUCUMBERS

1 large salad cucumber or 3 or 4 small pickling cucumbers
1 1/2 tsp. umeboshi vinegar
1/4 cup red onion, finely sliced

- Wash cucumber, and peel if waxed or oiled. Slice lengthwise if large. Slice into thin rounds or half circles.
- Place onions in a vegetable press, and sprinkle with half the vinegar. Add the cucumbers and the rest of the vinegar.
- Apply pressure and press for 15 minutes.
- Remove from press and serve as a vegetable side dish, saving the liquid.

SCALLION-MISO CONDIMENT

1 bunch of scallions, washed and sliced, including roots (about 1 cup)
1 tsp. barley miso
toasted sesame oil

- Heat a small skillet and brush with oil.
- Sauté scallion roots for 1 minute and then add scallions. Sauté for 1 minute and sprinkle with a little water.
- Mix miso in 2 tsp. of water and place on top of scallions, cover, and simmer for just 3 minutes. Stir and serve over grain, noodles, or vegetables.

Day 6

Breakfast

Soft Millet and Onions
Miso Soup
Nori Condiment

SOFT MILLET AND ONIONS

leftover millet
water
1/2 cup sunflower seeds or walnuts

- Prepare millet as in breakfast cereal (*see Day 2*).
- Wash seeds or nuts and let drain in a strainer while pan heats.
- Heat a heavy stainless steel frying pan, add seeds, and toast on a medium-low flame, stirring constantly until they are lightly browned (about 10 minutes).
- Serve seeds (or nuts) over cereal.
- Store in a dry jar after cooling.

MISO SOUP

2-inch piece of wakame
1/2 cup onions, sliced
1/2 cup cauliflower, sliced
1/4 cup tofu, diced
4 to 5 cups water
2 to 3 tsp. brown rice miso
several carrot flowers
parsley for garnish

- Rinse wakame, soak for a few minutes, and cut up.
- Bring water, wakame, and onions to a boil. Add cauliflower, tofu, and carrots.
- Return to a boil, lower flame, and simmer for 3 minutes.
- Dilute miso in a little water and add to soup, simmering for 3 more minutes.
- Serve with garnish.

Steam or boil some greens for breakfast

NORI CONDIMENT

5 or 6 pieces of nori cut into 1-inch-square pieces
several drops of shoyu

• Put nori in a small sauce pan with enough water to cover nori.
• Bring to a boil, reduce flame to low, and simmer covered until most of the water evaporates and nori forms a thick paste, about 20 minutes. (Use a flame deflector if pan is thin.)
• Add shoyu a few minutes before the end of cooking time.
• Serve over grains or noodles.

Lunch

Noodle Rolls
Quick Stir Fry
Aduki Soup

NOODLE ROLLS

$1/2$ lb. somen or soba noodles
several scallions, cut into 7-inch-long strips
carrot, cut into several 7-inch-long strips
cucumber, cut thinly into 7-inch-long strips
toasted nori sheets
umeboshi paste
brown rice vinegar

• Boil a large pan of water.
• Divide noodles into 4 bundles and tie a piece of string firmly around one end of each bundle. Drop into boiling water and cook until done (still slightly firm).
• Drain gently and rinse. Drain again. Cut off string and hard ends of noodles that were under the string. (Recook and eat hard pieces.)
• Place a sheet of nori on a bamboo sushi mat.

- Evenly spread a bundle of noodles over nori.
- Blanch carrots and drain well. Optional: blanch scallions.
- Along one long end, place a strip of carrot, scallion, and cucumber. Spread a small amount of umeboshi paste along noodles in the middle of the sheet. Sprinkle with vinegar.
- Roll up, starting with the end containing vegetables. (This will be the center of the roll when done.) Squeeze roll with mat as you roll it up, lifting the mat after each squeeze so it does not get caught in the roll !
- Slice the roll into 4 or 5 equal size pieces with a sharp wet knife. Start cutting in the center of the roll and work out toward the ends.
- Place on a platter to serve.

QUICK STIR FRY

1 onion, sliced into thin half moons
bok choy, several leaves sliced into $1/2$-inch diagonals
1 cup edible pea pods, sliced into $1/2$-inch diagonal slices or left whole
1 Tbs. toasted sesame oil or olive (can be water-sautéed)
few drops shoyu

- Heat a wok or frying pan, add oil or 2 Tbs. water, and when hot add onions. Sauté for 5 minutes on a high flame, stirring constantly. Add bok choy and pea pods, sprinkle with shoyu, and sauté a few minutes or just until pea pods are bright green.
- Place in a serving dish and serve warm.

ADUKI SOUP

1 cup leftover aduki beans
3 cups water or any saved vegetable cooking water
$1/4$ cup dried elbow or shell pasta
sliced parsley for garnish

- Mix beans into water and bring to a boil, stir in pasta, and simmer until pasta is soft. Garnish and serve.

Dinner

Sweet Rice with Chestnuts
Lentil Stew
Sautéed Vegetables
Sea Palm
Quick Boiled Greens
Red Radish Umeboshi Pickles

SWEET RICE WITH CHESTNUTS

2 cups sweet brown rice
$1/2$ cup dried chestnuts
3 to 4 cups water
2 pinches sea salt

• Sort and wash rice, wash chestnuts, and soak together in measured water for 3 to 5 hours or overnight.
• Place in a pressure cooker with salt, and mix gently. Cook under pressure 45 to 50 minutes. Let pressure come down naturally.

LENTIL STEW

$3/4$ cup dried green lentils
1 2-inch strip kombu
1 cup leeks, finely sliced on a diagonal
1 cup winter or yellow summer squash (whichever is in season)
1 tsp. mellow barley miso
3 to 4 cups of water
sliced scallion or chive for garnish

• Place kombu in a heavy soup pot, place leeks in next, then squash, and put lentils on top of vegetables. Gently pour water down side of pot.
• Cover and bring to a boil on a medium flame, lower flame, and

simmer until lentils are soft, 45 to 60 minutes, adding more water if needed. Do not stir.
• Place miso on top, cover, and simmer for 5 minutes. Stir well and serve with garnish.

SAUTEED VEGETABLES

1 large onion, sliced into half-moon pieces
$1/2$ lb. fresh mushroom, cleaned and sliced
2 stalks celery, sliced thin on a diagonal
1 Tbs. olive or corn oil
1 tsp. shoyu
1 or 2 cloves of garlic, sliced (optional)

• Heat a skillet, add oil, add onions, and sauté on a medium flame for a few minutes.
• Add mushrooms and sauté for about 5 minutes. Add celery and garlic and sauté for a few more minutes.
• Add a little water and shoyu. Cover pan, lower flame, and simmer for 5 minutes.

SEA PALM

1 cup dried sea palm
1 cup cauliflower flowerettes
1 tsp. brown rice vinegar
1 tsp. shoyu

• Rinse sea palm and soak for 5 minutes, discard soaking water, and cut sea palm into 1- or 2-inch-long pieces.
• Place sea palm in a pot with enough water to just cover. Cover pot and bring to a boil, lower flame, and simmer 10 minutes.
• Place cauliflower on top of sea palm, cover, and cook about 3 minutes. Add shoyu and vinegar and cook 5 more minutes.
• For a richer tasting dish mix 2 tsp. tahini with shoyu and stir into sea palm with vinegar.
• Stir and serve.

QUICK BOILED GREENS

• Use a dark green leafy vegetable that you haven't used for at least four days or use up small pieces of different greens that need to be used up along with any pea pods, squash, or other leftovers.
• Prepare and cook, using quick boiling methods described previously. Cook each vegetable separately and adjust the length of time to make them soft but still slightly crisp and bright green.

RED RADISH UMEBOSHI PICKLE

10 to 12 umeboshi pits or 1 tsp. umeboshi flesh cut into small pieces
1 cup water
$1/3$ cup red radishes, sliced

• Place pits or plum in water and bring to a boil, simmer for 15 minutes, and let cool.
• Remove pits and pour liquid over radishes in a bowl or jar. Cover with a piece of cheesecloth and let sit for one to three days until radishes are soft and red. The thinner the radishes are sliced, the quicker they will pickle.
• Refrigerate. Liquid can be saved for use in cooking or in a dressing.

Day 7

Breakfast

Mochi Pancakes
Miso Soup

MOCHI PANCAKES

1/4 lb. packaged mochi per person
corn oil
few drops of shoyu

- Grate mochi on a cheese grater (some brands are very hard and dry and can only be crumbled or cut up).
- Heat a heavy frying pan, brush with oil, and on a low flame place 2 Tbs. of grated mochi. Add a few drops of shoyu to each pile of mochi. Cover pan and allow to melt.
- Serve plain, with apple butter, or with sautéed vegetables.

MISO SOUP

2 shiitake mushrooms, rinsed, soaked, and finely sliced
2-inch piece of wakame, rinsed, soaked, and cut up
3-inch piece of daikon, sliced into thin rounds, then into matchsticks
2 leaves nappa cabbage, finely sliced
2 tsp. barley miso
sliced chives for garnish

- Boil shiitake and wakame in water and simmer 5 minutes.
- Add vegetables and simmer for 3 minutes.
- Dilute miso in a little water, stir into soup, and simmer 3 more minutes. Serve with garnish.

Lunch

Lentil Patties
Sea Palm Salad
Marinated Cucumbers
Rice Pudding

LENTIL PATTIES

1 cup leftover lentil stew (strain out any liquid)
$1/4$ cup parsley, minced
whole wheat pastry flour
corn oil

• Grind lentils in a suribachi to break up squash pieces and mix in parsley. Add just enough flour to form patties that hold together.
• Heat a skillet and brush with oil. Cook patties on a medium flame until lightly browned on both sides. Press them down slightly with a spatula so they will cook all the way through.
• Serve with a dab of prepared, natural mustard or a little sauerkraut.

SEA PALM SALAD

1 cup or less leftover sea palm
1 tsp. tahini or 1 Tbs. roasted brown sesame seeds crushed
2 tsp. umeboshi vinegar or 1 Tbs. liquid from making red
   radish pickles plus $1/2$ tsp. umeboshi paste
$1/4$ cup chives or scallions, minced

• Mix tahini and liquid well and heat on a low flame for a few minutes. Cool and stir in chives. Mix into sea palm and chill.

MARINATED CUCUMBERS

1 salad cucumber or a few pickling cukes
$1/4$ cup mung bean sprouts (optional)
2 Tbs. brown rice vinegar
1 tsp. shoyu
1 Tbs. water

• Wash and slice cucumber into thin rounds. Peel if waxed or oiled.
• Mix shoyu, water, and vinegar; pour over cucumbers in a bowl; and let sit for about one hour.
• Drain off liquid and save. Serve cukes at room temp or chilled.

RICE PUDDING

1 cup leftover rice with chestnuts
1 Tbs. raisins or currants
1 Tbs. rice syrup or barley malt

Optional for a richer dessert:
1 tsp. tahini
$1/4$ tsp. cinnamon
$1/4$ tsp. vanilla extract

• Mix all ingredients
• Heat on a low flame over a flame deflector. Stir often.
• Cook for 5 minutes, and serve plain or with roasted chopped walnuts or almonds.

Dinner

Soba Noodles
Shiitake-Scallion Broth with Instant Kombu
Tempura Vegetables with Dip

SOBA NOODLES

1 lb. soba (buckwheat noodles)
a few drops of olive oil

• Substitute udon or somen during warm weather.
• Use soba for active young people and adults. Substitute wheat noodles or soy spaghetti for small children or for those watching their salt intake.
• Boil a large pot of water (and add oil for wheat pasta). Add noodles and stir.
• When water comes to a boil, add a little cold water, just enough to stop the boiling, and stir. Repeat two more times.
• Soba noodles usually cook in under 10 minutes and need to be rinsed after draining to remove some of the salt. Do not save salty

cooking water.
• Place noodles on a serving platter, or if using two different kinds, put them side by side on the same platter.

SHIITAKE-SCALLION BROTH WITH INSTANT KOMBU

2 large or 4 small shiitake mushrooms, rinsed and soaked until soft

4 scallions
4 cups water
1 to 2 Tbs. shoyu
1 to 2 Tbs. instant kombu (a processed kombu that contains rice vinegar and is ready to use; also called *tororo kombu* and available through some mail-order companies)
a few raw scallion slices

• Bring water, shiitake, and shiitake soaking water to a boil. Cook for a few minutes, then remove shiitake, slice them finely, and return pieces to the broth with desired amount of shoyu. Simmer for 15 minutes.
• Wash and slice scallions into 2-inch-long pieces. Thick white ends should be cut in half lengthwise. Thick white ends should be cut in half lengthwise.
• Serve broth over noodles in individual bowls with a little of the instant kombu and raw scallion.
• Optional: Simmer diced tofu in the broth with scallion pieces.

TEMPURAED VEGETABLES WITH DIP

1 or more of the following vegetables: onion rounds, broccoli flowers, thin slices of winter squash and carrots, sprigs of parsley, scallions (a good time to use up pieces of vegetables accumulating in the refrigerator)

Batter:
1/2 cup whole wheat pastry flour
1/2 cup unbleached white flour or corn flour
1/4 tsp. sea salt
1 level Tbs. arrowroot flour diluted in a little water
1 cup water (for a party, try carbonated water or beer instead of regular water)

• Mix dry ingredients. Gently mix in water until batter is smooth, but do not overmix or you will activate the gluten in the flour and the coating will be doughy instead of crisp.
• Keep batter cool. If separated from vegetables when dropped into oil, add a little more flour to the batter.
• Toasted sesame oil, safflower oil, or a mixture of the two oils can be used. Heat 2 inches in a wok or heavy pot. Oil is ready when a drop of batter placed in it rises slowly to the top. If it stays at the bottom, the oil is not hot enough. If it does not sink and then rises, the oil is too hot.
• Dip vegetables in batter and place a few slices in the oil at a time, cooking them for a few minutes on each side until golden and crisp. Drain well. Tip: Use separate utensils for putting vegetables in and out of the batter so end of the utensils remain unsticky.
• Cool oil, strain, and store in the refrigerator covered in a glass jar. Odors (especially from fish) and oil can be cleaned out by dropping an umeboshi into hot oil and cooking it until it is charred.

Dipping sauce:
1Tbs. shoyu
1Tbs. water
a few drops ginger juice
1 tsp. brown rice vinegar (optional)

• Heat water and shoyu for a few minutes on a low flame, cool, and add vinegar and ginger juice.
• Optional: 1 Tbs. grated daikon per person sprinkled with umeboshi vinegar can be served to aid digestion of tempura (or any heavy or oily food).

Week 2

Day 8

Breakfast

Whole Wheat Couscous Cereal
Miso Soup with Shredded Kombu
Steamed Greens

WHOLE WHEAT COUSCOUS CEREAL

1 cup whole wheat couscous
1 onion, sliced into thin half moons
3 cups water
1/4 tsp. shoyu

• Boil water and stir in onions and couscous. Lower flame and simmer 10 minutes, adding more water as it cooks if too dry. Add shoyu and simmer for 5 more minutes.

MISO SOUP WITH SHREDDED KOMBU

4 cups water
1 carrot, sliced into thin rounds and then cut into fine matchsticks
1/3 cup lotus root, cut into thin rounds, then cut in half
2 Tbs. shredded kombu (a processed flavored quick cooking kombu also called *natto kombu*)
2 tsp. brown rice miso
sliced scallion for garnish

- Bring water to a boil with carrot and lotus root, add kombu, and simmer for about 5 minutes. Dilute and add miso, simmering for 3 more minutes. Serve with garnish.

STEAMED GREENS

kale or collard greens, 1/4 to 1/2 cup raw per person

Dressing:
2 tsp. umeboshi paste
1/2 cup roasted pumpkin seeds
1 Tbs. parsley, mincedzk
1 Tbs. fresh lemon juice
3/4 cup water

- Wash greens carefully and cut stems from leaves. Slice stem into desired lengths.
- Slice leaves into strips or squares.
- Steam as in previous recipes, cooking stems and leaves separately and only until bright green.
- Grind seeds finely and grind in remaining ingredients. Serve over greens.

Lunch

Crepes
Vegetable Topping
Pressed Nappa and Bean Sprouts

CREPES

2 1/2 cups whole wheat pastry flour
1/2 cup kuzu (or 3/4 cup arrowroot flour; the result is better with kuzu)
3 cups cold water

1 pinch of sea salt
corn oil

• Dilute kuzu or arrowroot in cold water.
• Combine the rest of the ingredients except oil. Mix well.
• Heat a crepe pan or small skillet and brush with oil. Add $1/4$ cup of batter at a time, quickly lifting and tilting pan to evenly spread batter. Cook over medium low flame for about 3 minutes. Flip crepe over and cook for a few minutes on the other side.
• The crepes can be served with a desert topping, e.g., lemon sauce or cooked, fresh, or dried fruit.

VEGETABLE TOPPING

1 onion, sliced into thin half moons
1 carrot, sliced into thin matchsticks
$1/4$ cup burdock root, sliced into thin matchsticks
$1/4$ cup lotus root, sliced into thin half circles
2 Tbs. olive, toasted sesame oil, or water for sautéeing
1 $1/2$ cups water
1 tsp. shoyu

• Heat a wok or cast-iron skillet, add oil, and lower flame to medium.
• Add onions and sauté for 5 minutes, add burdock and sauté for 5 more minutes, and add carrots and lotus and continue sautéeing for 5 more minutes.
• Add water, cover, and simmer for 10 minutes.
• Dilute kuzu in a little cold water, stir in kuzu, sprinkle with shoyu, and stir until liquid thickens.
• Serve over crepes.
• Optional: Spring and summer vegetables could be leaks, string beans, peas, or pea pods.

PRESSED NAPPA AND BEAN SPROUTS

1 1/2 cups nappa cabbage leaves, washed and thinly sliced
1/2 cup mung bean sprouts, rinsed
2 tsp. sea salt
1 tsp. shiso leaf powder, green nori flakes, or roasted ground dulse

- In a bowl, mix cabbage, sprouts, and salt.
- Gently rub salt into vegetables, place in a vegetable press, and secure lid. Press for 10 minutes. (If no liquid comes out of vegetables after 10 minutes, pieces were cut too large. Add a little more salt and press for 5 more minutes.)
- Remove vegetables from press, drain through a strainer, saving the liquid to cook with (remembering that it is salty).
- Rinse vegetables well to remove any salt taste.
- Sprinkle with shiso, nori, or dulse.
- Serve at room temperature or cool.

Dinner

Rice with Black Soybeans
Barley Stew
Sautéed Cabbage
Squash with Wakame
Boiled Salad
Tofu Dressing

RICE WITH BLACK SOYBEANS

2 cups medium grain brown rice
1/4 cup soybeans
3 1/2 to 4 cups water
2 pinches of sea salt

- Clean soybeans by rolling them gently several times in a damp cotton towel.

- Wash rice and let sit in a strainer. Roast soybeans in a hot, dry, heavy skillet, stirring constantly on a medium low flame for 10 minutes or until they are dry, the skins begin to crack, and beans are lightly browned evenly.
- Place beans, rice, and water in a pressure cooker on a low flame for 10 minutes.
- Add salt, secure lid, and bring up to pressure on a high flame. Cook under pressure for 55 minutes.
- Remove and mix well.

BARLEY STEW

2 cups dried whole barley, washed and soaked in 6 cups of water for 6 to 8 hours
2 pinches of sea salt
1/4 cup sliced vegetables chosen from among the following: leeks, celery, carrots, rutabaga, burdock, and seitan
1 tsp. sweet miso
celery leaves or chives for garnish

- Pressure cook barley with soaking water and salt for 1 hour.
- Save half the barley for the next day's breakfast.
- In a soup pot, layer vegetables in the order listed above with seitan on top, then barley. (Any leftover beans also can be added as well as dried tofu or fu.)
- Gently add water to the pot to cover barley, plus two or three inches. Cover pot and bring to a boil on a medium flame. Lower flame and simmer for 25 minutes.
- Dilute miso, add to soup, and simmer for 5 minutes.
- Stir and serve with garnish.

SAUTEED CABBAGE

3 cups green or red cabbage, finely sliced
1 Tbs. corn or toasted sesame oil
2 tsp. umeboshi paste

- Heat a skillet or wok and add oil. Add cabbage and sauté on a me-

dium heat for 10 minutes.
• Mix paste in a little water and place on top of cabbage, cover, lower flame, and simmer for a few minutes. Stir well and serve warm.

SQUASH WITH WAKAME

1 3-inch strip of wakame, rinsed and soaked a few minutes then cut into 1-inch pieces
1 $1/2$ cups diced winter squash or yellow summer squash
shoyu

• Place wakame followed by squash in a saucepan, add 1 inch of water ($1/2$ inch for summer squash), sprinkle with a little shoyu, cover, and bring to a boil.
•Lower flame and simmer 5 minutes or until squash is soft.

BOILED SALAD

1 cup broccoli, sliced
4 leaves bok choy
$1/2$ cup daikon, sliced

• Cook as in previous recipe for quick boiled salad, drain well, and arrange attractively on a platter. Save cooking water.

TOFU DRESSING

$1/2$ lb. soft tofu
1 Tbs. tahini
1 Tbs. onion, minced or grated
1 tsp. sweet miso
1 $1/2$ Tbs. brown rice vinegar
$3/4$ cup water from boiling vegetables

• Blend all ingredients, heat for a few minutes on a low flame, cool, and serve over salad.

Day 9

Breakfast

Shoyu Soup
Soft Barley with Vegetables
Steamed Pea Pods

SHOYU SOUP

1 Tbs. dry dulse, rinsed
1 cup nappa, savoy, or Chinese cabbage, thinly sliced
2 to 3 tsp. shoyu
carrot for garnish, finely grated

- Bring water and cabbage to a boil.
- Cut up dulse and add along with shoyu. Simmer soup for 5 minutes.
- Serve in individual bowls and garnish.

SOFT BARLEY WITH VEGETABLES

leftover barley
water
diced vegetables (e.g., onions, carrots, celery, squash and/or corn cut off the cob)

- Mix desired amount of water and vegetables into barley and simmer until water is absorbed and vegetables are soft.

STEAMED PEA PODS

1 cup edible pea pods (snow peas) or any quick cooking green vegetable

- Wash and remove stems from pods. Steam until bright green, less than 1 minute.
- Serve with soup or cereal.

Lunch

Nori Rolls
Barley Stew with Croutons
Watercress

NORI ROLLS

leftover black soy bean rice (steam if hard or dry)
toasted nori sheets
cucumber, thinly sliced
umeboshi paste
brown rice vinegar

- Place a sheet of nori on a sushi mat. With a wet rice paddle, spread 1 or 2 cups of rice on the nori, leaving a little space around the edges,
- Place a cucumber strip lengthwise, about $1/2$ inch from the bottom of the sheet of nori.
- Spread a little paste along the cucumber and sprinkle with a little vinegar.
- Roll up the nori using the mat to press it firmly as you roll.
- If needed, wet the edge of the nori slightly to seal the rolled up sushi.
- Slice into 5 or 6 rounds with a wet sharp knife, starting in the center of the roll and cutting out to both ends.
- Arrange on a platter with cut sides up.
- Try other ingredients: various types of pickles, cooked or raw vegetables, tofu, tempeh or seitan, or sesame seeds.

BARLEY STEW WITH CROUTONS

leftover stew
$1/2$ cup whole wheat sourdough bread, cubed
1 Tbs. olive or sesame oil
1 tsp. shoyu
2 tsp. minced parsley
pinch of oregano

- Heat stew.
- Mix all ingredients together to make croutons. Cook in a small skillet, stirring constantly for 5 minutes on a medium flame or place under a broiler for 3 minutes.
- Serve croutons in stew with a raw garnish.

WATERCRESS

1 bunch watercress, untied and washed carefully

- Drop a few sprigs of watercress at a time into shallow boiling water. Cook for 1 minute or less, drain well, and serve whole or cut up.

Dinner

Carrot Soup
Bulgur with Wakame
Vegetable Stew
Double Cooked String Beans
Baked Tofu
Lemon-Miso Sauce

CARROT SOUP

2 cups carrots, sliced
3 cups water
1 pinch of sea salt

chives, sliced
- Steam carrots over 2 cups of water with salt. Purée carrots, and mix into cooking water, adding an extra cup of water. Simmer for 15 minutes. Garnish with chives.

BULGUR WITH WAKAME

1 １/₂ cups bulgur
3 cups water
a pinch of sea salt
leftover wakame
a pinch of dry mustard powder and a little brown rice vinegar (optional)

- Boil water and salt. Add bulgur and stir.
- Return to a boil, lower flame, and simmer for 15 minutes. (Some types of bulgur are more processed than others and require less or no cooking time. Just stir into boiling water, cover, and let sit until water is absorbed.)
- Stir in wakame dish and simmer for 3 minutes with seasonings.

VEGETABLE STEW

2 small onions, cut into quarters
4 wedges of head cabbage about 1 １/₂ inches-thick on the outside edge
8 Brussels sprouts, washed, hard ends cut off, and sliced in half
shoyu
１/₄ cup brown rice flour (optional)

- Place vegetables in a saucepan with 2 inches of water. Cover and bring to a boil.
- Lower flame and simmer until vegetables are done (about 5 minutes).
- Sprinkle with shoyu and simmer for 3 more minutes or gently scoop out vegetables into a bowl. Stir shoyu and flour into remaining liquid and simmer, stirring often until the stew thickens and pour over vegetables.

DOUBLE COOKED STRING BEANS

2 cups string beans, washed and stems removed
½ cup toasted brown sesame seeds crushed in a suribachi
1 Tbs. toasted sesame oil
1½ tsp. shoyu

- Cut string beans into 2-inch-long pieces or leave whole, and steam until almost done.
- Heat a skillet, oil, and add string beans and shoyu.
- Sauté on a medium flame for a few minutes, and stir in sesame seeds while sautéeing.
- Serve warm.

BAKED TOFU

1 lb. tofu
toasted sesame oil or corn oil

- Brush a baking pan with oil and heat oven to 350 degrees. Slice tofu into four pieces.
- Place tofu into pan, cover, and bake for 10 minutes.
- If you wish to avoid baking, follow same directions using a heavy covered skillet on top of the stove.

MISO-LEMON SAUCE

2 or 3 Tbs. fresh lemon juice
1 tsp. barley miso
1 Tbs. water
1 Tbs. scallions, sliced

- Mix lemon juice and miso into water, heat on a low flame for a few minutes, and stir in scallions as it cooks.
- Serve a small amount on each piece of tofu. The sauce is also good on noodles or crisply cooked vegetables.

Day 10

Breakfast

Scrambled Tofu
Miso Soup
Corn Bread

SCRAMBLED TOFU

1 lb. soft tofu, crumbled
corn oil or water
$1/2$ cup onions, diced
$1/2$ cup corn, cut off the cob
umeboshi vinegar
$1/4$ cup scallions, sliced

- Heat a small amount of oil in a skillet. Sauté onions for a few minutes.
- Stir in corn, place tofu on top, cover, and simmer for 5 minutes.
- Add a little vinegar and scallions, and simmer for a few more minutes.

MISO SOUP

3-inch piece of wakame, rinsed, soaked, and cut up
4 to 5 cups water
1 onion, sliced into thin half moons
2 tsp. sesame oil
$2 1/2$ tsp. barley miso
raw garnish

- Bring water and wakame to a boil.
- Heat a skillet with oil, sauté onions for a few minutes, and add to

soup.
- Simmer for a few minutes, add diluted miso, and simmer for a few more minutes.
- Garnish with chives, scallions, or parsley

CORNBREAD

1 1/2 cup cornmeal
1/2 cup whole wheat pastry flour
a pinch of sea salt
1 1/2 cups hot water
3 Tbs. corn oil
2 Tbs barley malt or brown rice syrup
corn oil for the pan
1/2 cup corn kernels, diced onions or raisins, a pinch of cinnamon (optional)

- Preheat oven to 300 degrees.
- Brush a 9-inch cast-iron skillet with oil and place in oven until very hot but not smoking.
- In a bowl, mix dry ingredients. In another bowl, mix wet ingredients. Mix together and stir in any optional ingredients.
- Pour batter into hot skillet and bake 30 minutes or until done in the center. Cornbread will dry out as it cools. If recipe is doubled, it will need to cook longer.
- As an alternative to baking, you may place skillet on to burner with a flame deflector under it and a heavy, tight-fitting lid on top. Cook on a very low flame for 1 hour.

Lunch

Pasta with String Beans
Natto Soy Beans
Vegetable Stew

PASTA WITH STRING BEANS

½ lb. whole wheat, artichoke, corn, or a light variety of pasta, elbows, or shells
leftover string beans

- Cook pasta until done but still firm, drain, and stir string beans into pasta.
- Steam or lightly stir fry for a few minutes to blend flavors.

Heat leftover vegetable stew in a covered sauce pan on a low flame until warm.

NATTO SOYBEANS

1 container of natto soy beans (6 oz.)
2 scallions, finely sliced
a pinch of dry mustard powder
¼ tsp. shoyu
¼ tsp. ginger juice, fresh grated

- Place soybeans on a very wet cutting board and cut into small pieces.
- Mix in remaining ingredients well.
- Let sit for at least 15 minutes before serving

Heat leftover vegetable stew on low flame until warm.

Dinner

Boiled Basmati and Wild Rice
Pan Cooked White Fish
Water Sautéed Onions And Carrots
Raw Salad
Herb Dressing
Quick Pressed Pickles

BOILED BASMATI AND WILD RICE

3/4 cup brown basmati rice
1/4 cup wild rice
2 cups water
1/2 tsp. shoyu

- Boil water in a heavy pot
- Wash rices separately and let sit in strainers. Heat a skillet and roast rices separately, basmati until lightly golden in color and wild rice until just dry.
- Add rices and shoyu to boiling water, cover, and return to a boil.
- Lower flame and simmer for 1 hour.
- Stir gently when done.

WHITE FISH

1/4 lb. or less fish per person
juice of 1 lemon
shoyu
olive oil

- Brush a skillet with oil and heat, place fish in pan, cover, and simmer for a few minutes.
- Mix juice with a little water and shoyu, pour over fish, and simmer for a few minutes.
- Fish is done when it flakes easily with a fork. Do not overcook. Prepare after other dishes so it can be eaten as soon as it is done.

WATER SAUTEED ONIONS AND CARROTS

2 small onions, sliced into fine half moons
1 carrot, sliced into fine matchsticks
2 Tbs. water

a pinch of sea salt
sprinkle of shoyu

- Heat a skillet, add water, and when hot add onions and carrots.
- Sprinkle with salt and sauté on a medium flame until almost done. Add shoyu and sauté for 3 more minutes.
- Optional: Use bok choy instead of carrots in warm weather.

RAW SALAD

1 small head dark green leaf lettuce
red radish, grated
cucumber, sliced
red onion, finely sliced
raw sprouts

- Toss desired amounts of each ingredient together and keep salad cool until ready to use.

HERB DRESSING

1 cup liquid saved from homemade brine pickles or purchased pickles or sauerkraut
1 Tbs. olive oil
2 Tbs. apple cider vinegar
1 Tbs. parsley, minced (including stems)
2 Tbs. cucumber, minced
1 Tbs. scallion or onion, sliced
1 tsp. fresh or dried dill weed

- Mix oil and vinegar into water and heat on a low flame for a few minutes. Do not boil.
- Let cool and then blend with remaining ingredients.
- Serve over individual salads and save extra salad and dressing for later.

QUICK PRESSED PICKLES

1 cup daikon, thinly sliced and then slivered
1 1/2 tsp. sea salt

• Mix salt into daikon and rub it in with hands for a few minutes.
• Press in a vegetable press for 3 hours or all day.
• When done, rinse under cold water and serve.
• The pickles will keep about 1 to 2 weeks if stored in the refrigerator.

Day 11

Breakfast

Steamed Bread
Onion Butter
Homemade Rice Kayu Bread

STEAMED BREAD

whole wheat sourdough or rye bread

• Steam thick slices of bread until soft.

ONION BUTTER

6 to 8 cups onions, sliced or diced

• Optional: Sauté onions in a little corn or sesame oil for 5 minutes.
• Place onions and a pinch of sea salt in a pressure cooker with a little water.
• Cook under pressure for about 5 minutes. Remove from cooker

and put onions through a hand food mill.
• Put puréed onions in a heavy pot and simmer for 1 to 2 hours, stirring occasionally. Use a flame deflector. The onion butter is done when it is cooked down into a thick paste and is sweet.
• Serve on bread or rice cakes.

STEAMED RICE KAYU BREAD

1 cup leftover rice or other grain
2 cups water saved from cooking noodles, making seitan, cooking vegetables, or plain
4 to 5 cups whole wheat bread flour
2 Tbs. corn oil (optional)

• Dough will rise more if liquid is slightly sour or add 1 tsp. miso to kayu.
• Pressure cook rice and water for 10 minutes or simmer for 30 minutes. Let cool.
• This mixture is called *kayu*, and it can be used as is or put through a food mill or blender to purée the rice pieces.
• Put kayu in a large bowl. Mix in miso and oil (if using oil). Mix in flour a little at a time until dough holds together well.
• Flour hands and knead dough, adding more flour if needed to keep dough from sticking to hands or sides of the bowl.
• Knead until dough is soft and elastic; it cannot be overkneaded.
• Place in a clean, lightly oiled bowl. The top of the dough can be lightly oiled to keep it soft.
• Cover with a damp cloth and let sit in a warm place for 8 to 12 hours.
• Gently form into small loaf shapes and cook in a steamer basket for 1 hour. Check water level often. If you have a large steamer, dough can be put into loaf pans, and pans can be placed in steamer. Cook for 1 $1/2$ hours if making in pans.
• Bread will be wet when done and will dry out as it cools. Store in a refrigerator.

Lunch

Stuffed Cabbage
Miso-Tahini Sauce
Corn on the Cob

STUFFED CABBAGE

6 to 8 savoy cabbage leaves
leftover rice or other grain
leftover beans or natto
leftover onions and carrots
$1/4$ cup parsley or scallions, sliced

- Steam cabbage leaves until flexible.
- Mix leftovers and parsley.
- Place $1/4$ to $1/2$ cup of the mixture in the center of each leaf.
- Fold ends in and roll up.
- Place in a steamer basket and steam for 5 minutes.
- Keep warm until ready to serve.

MISO-TAHINI SAUCE

2 Tbs. tahini
2 tsp. sweet miso
1 tsp. brown rice vinegar
2 Tbs. water from steaming cabbage

- Mix ingredients together well.
- Heat on a low flame for 5 minutes, stirring constantly.
- Place a small amount on each cabbage roll.

CORN ON THE COB

½ to 1 ear per person
2 Tbs. corn oil
1 tsp. umeboshi paste

• Steam corn for 3 to 5 minutes.
• Mix umeboshi paste in the corn oil and heat for 5 minutes on a very low flame. Cool and brush or spread a little on each ear of corn.

Dinner

Millet Loaf
Squash Sauce
Great Northern Beans
Hiziki with Dried Daikon and Leeks
Green Rolls
Pickled Collard Stems

MILLET LOAF

2 cups dried millet
6 cups of water
a pinch of sea salt

• Boil water and salt.
• Wash millet and add to boiling water, return to a boil, lower flame, and simmer for 25 minutes.
• While still hot, place millet in a cake or bread pan and press down lightly. Let sit until it hardens.
• Slice and serve millet loaf as is, or broil or pan fry slices sprinkled with a little shoyu in a little oil to reheat.
• Optional: Wrap a ½-inch-wide strip of nori around each slice.

SQUASH SAUCE

2 cups winter squash, cubed (use carrots or cauliflower if squash is not in season)
1 tsp. sweet miso
2 tsp. tahini or nut butter (optional)
scallions, sliced

- Steam squash.
- Put through a hand food mill or food processor, do not add water unless too dry to purée.
- Blend in miso and tahini.
- Cook on a low flame, stirring constantly for 5 minutes. Serve over millet loaf with a scallion garnish.

GREAT NORTHERN BEANS

1 cup dry beans, washed and soaked in 3 cups of water 4 hours or overnight
1 small onion, diced
1/4 cup parsnip, diced
1/4 cup carrot, diced
2 Tbs. burdock root, slivered
1 2-inch strip kombu
2 tsp. sweet miso

- Clean kombu and place in a heavy pot.
- Place beans and soaking water in pot, cover, and bring to a boil.
- Lower flame and simmer for 1 $1/2$ to 2 hours, longer for easier digestibility. Add water as needed to keep water level just to the top of the beans. Do not stir.
- Layer vegetables on top of beans in the following order: onions, parsnips, carrots, burdock. Gently push them down into beans a little.
- Add water to almost cover beans if needed. Cover and simmer for 30 minutes or until burdock is soft.
- Place miso on top of beans and simmer for 5 more minutes. Do not

add more water after adding miso.
- If beans are too watery, cook with lid off for a few minutes.
- Gently stir, cover, and let sit until ready to serve.

HIZIKI WITH DRIED DAIKON AND LEEKS

1/4 cup dried hiziki, rinsed and soaked for 15 minutes
2 tsp. toasted sesame oil
1/4 cup dry daikon, rinsed and soaked 15 to 30 minutes
1 cup leeks, washed and soaked
shoyu

- Heat a skillet and add oil.
- Drain hiziki, discard liquid, and slice hiziki into 1-inch-long pieces. Put in skillet and sauté on a medium low flame for 5 minutes.
- Drain daikon, discard liquid if dark in color, cut up daikon, and place on top of hiziki.
- Place leeks on top of daikon.
- Add enough water, including daikon soaking water if light, to just cover the hiziki.
- Cover pan and bring to a boil. Simmer for 45 minutes, adjusting the time as necessary depending on the thickness of hiziki. Add more water if needed during first half hour of cooking time.
- Sprinkle with shoyu and simmer 5 more minutes.
- Stir before serving.

GREEN ROLLS

4 whole nappa cabbage leaves
4 collard leaves with stems cut out
4 thin carrot strips
slices of pickled shiso leaves, cucumber brine pickles, or sauerkraut

- Steam or boil leaves until flexible and the carrots until soft. Save liquid.

- Drain leaves and pat dry with a towel.
- Place a cabbage leaf on a collard leaf and lay a carrot strip and a slice of shiso leaf across the cabbage leaf so that they span the width of the leaf.
- Starting from the base of the leaf, roll up tightly to create a cylinder. Slice into rounds and place on a platter cut side up.
- Prepare half of the green rolls with a collard leaf on the outside and half with a cabbage leaf on the inside. Any small end pieces that are cut off when slicing the cylinders can be put inside the next roll.
- Use the cooking water to make a kuzu sauce, adding a little shoyu, miso, or lemon juice to taste.

PICKLED COLLARD STEMS

collard stems (saved from previous recipe)
1/4 cup shoyu
1 Tbs. brown rice vinegar

- Cut washed stems into 1- or 2-inch-long diagonal pieces.
- Mix shoyu and brown rice vinegar. Umeboshi vinegar may be used instead of shoyu or mixed with the brown rice vinegar.
- Place stems in a bowl or jar and cover with liquid, place cheesecloth on top of container, and let sit for 4 to 8 hours.
- Rinse before eating, store in a refrigerator, and save liquid for new pickles or use in cooking.

Day 12

Breakfast

Layered Miso Soup
Corn Grits
Water-Sautéed Nappa

LAYERED MISO SOUP

1½ inch piece of wakame
1 onion, sliced into thin half moons
1 cup yellow summer squash, cut into small pieces
4 cups water
1½ tsp. brown rice miso
scallions, sliced

• Layer ingredients in pot in the following order: wakame, onions, squash.
• Gently pour water in, trying not to disturb the layering.
• Bring to a boil and simmer for 5 minutes.
• Stir in diluted miso and simmer for 3 minutes.
• Serve with garnish.

CORN GRITS

1 cup finely ground corn grits (some are coarsely ground, hard, and require soaking)
3 cups water
pinch of sea salt

• Boil water and salt. Stir in grits. Cover, return to a boil, and simmer for 20 minutes, stirring occasionally or until water is absorbed and grits are soft.

WATER-SAUTEED NAPPA

2 cups nappa or Chinese cabbage, sliced
2 Tbs. water
a pinch of sea salt

• Heat a skillet, add water and salt, when hot add cabbage, and sauté for 5 minutes, stirring constantly on a medium high flame.

Lunch

Pasta Salad
Sesame Umeboshi Dressing
Bean Spread
Greens
Homemade Sprouts

PASTA SALAD

2 cups cooked pasta (any type is suitable)
$1/4$ cup vegetables, steamed from among the following: broccoli, cauliflower, corn kernels
$1/4$ cup bean or alfalfa sprouts
$1/4$ leftover hiziki, drained well

• Mix pasta with cooked vegetables, rinsed sprouts and hiziki, add dressing, and chill.

SESAME UMEBOSHI DRESSING

$1/2$ cup toasted brown sesame seeds
2 tsp. brown rice vinegar
2 tsp. umeboshi paste
$1/4$ tsp. dill
$1/4$ cup cucumber, diced
$1/2$ cup plain water or liquid saved from cooking vegetables (do not use water from high mineral greens like kale or collards or bitter water from mustard or watercress)

• Crush seeds finely in a suribachi, blend with other ingredients, and chill.
• Stir dressing into pasta salad and keep cool until ready to serve.

BEAN SPREAD

1 cup leftover beans
1 tsp. tahini
1 tsp. umeboshi paste
1/4 cup chives or scallions, finely sliced
1 small onion, grated
1 Tbs. parsley, minced

• Mash all ingredients together in a suribachi or put through a hand food mill (you may need to add a little liquid to use the food mill).
• For easier digestibility, heat for a few minutes.
• Serve on bread or rice cakes.

Steam or boil some greens or nappa to go with lunch.

HOMEMADE SPROUTS

2 tsp. whole seeds, beans, or grains

• Wash seeds and place in a wide mouth glass jar, cover with water, cover the jar with cheesecloth, and secure with a rubber band.
• Let jar sit overnight in a dark place or in an open paper bag.
• Pour off liquid, rinse seeds, and drain well through cheesecloth.
• Rinse and drain seeds two times a day. Keep out of sunlight.
• They are ready to be eaten when sprouts are $1/4$-inch long, before roots appear.
• To get green leaves, place jar in sunlight after sprouts appear.
• Refrigerate when ready to use and rinse off any hard shells before eating. Use up in a few days, as they spoil quickly.

Dinner

Millet Soup
Nutty Rice
Squash Kanten
Stir Fried Vegetables with Tofu
Goma-Wakame Condiment
Greens

MILLET SOUP

1/4 cup leeks, sliced
1/4 cup celery, sliced
1/4 cup cauliflower, cut into pieces
1/4 cup millet, washed
5 cups water
a pinch of sea salt
2 tsp. shoyu or sweet white miso
celery leaves, scallions, or chives, sliced for garnish

- In a tall, narrow soup pot, layer ingredients as listed except for shoyu and garnish.
- Gently add water, cover, bring to a boil, and simmer for 25 minutes.
- Add shoyu or miso and simmer for 5 more minutes.
- Stir gently and serve with garnish.

NUTTY RICE

2 cups medium-grain brown rice, pressure-cooked or boiled as in any of the previous rice recipes using 1 or 2 tsp. shoyu instead of sea salt or kombu
1/3 cup walnuts

- Wash walnuts and drain well.
- Heat a skillet, add nuts, lower flame, and stir nut until dry and

lightly toasted evenly on all sides.
• Let nuts cool and then cut them up and stir into rice.

SQUASH KANTEN

2 cups butternut squash, diced (use carrots or any sweet combination of vegetables if squash are not in season)
1/4 cup onions
agar flakes
chives, sliced for garnish

• Use squash skins; if you wish to peel off skins because of color, save them and use in a soup or sauté.
• Steam squash until soft and blend with a little of the steaming water.
• Let cool and stir in onions and 1 heaping Tbs. agar agar flakes per cup of mixture.
• Stir well to dissolve flakes, bring to a boil, stirring often, and simmer for 5 minutes.
• Pour into a glass pan and let sit at room temperature for a half hour and then refrigerate until the kanten jells.
• Sprinkle with chives and cut into squares to serve.

STIR FRY VEGETABLES WITH TOFU

1 large sweet onion, sliced into fine half moons
1 1/2 cups broccoli, with the stems sliced into matchsticks and heads cut into tiny pieces
1 lb. firm tofu, diced
olive oil or sesame oil
clove of garlic, sliced
shoyu

• Heat a skillet or wok and add 2 Tbs. oil.
• Add onions and sauté on a medium flame for 10 minutes.
• Add broccoli, tofu, and garlic, and sauté for 5 minutes.
• Sprinkle with shoyu and sauté for 3 more minutes.

GOMA (SESAME) WAKAME CONDIMENT

1 cup brown or black sesame seeds
1/4 cup dry wakame

- Heat a heavy skillet, break up wakame, and place in skillet.
- Roast on a medium flame, stirring constantly until wakame crumbles easily.
- Grind wakame in a suribachi.
- Roast seeds as you would for gomashio and grind into wakame.
- When cool, store in an airtight jar. Serve over grains or vegetables or on salads.

Day 13

Breakfast

Whole Oats with Vegetables
Sesame-Shiso-Nori Condiment
Apple Fritters

WHOLE OATS WITH VEGETABLES

1 cup dried whole oat groats
3 1/2 cups water
1 onion, cut into quarters
1 parsnip, cut into 1/2-inch pieces
1 tsp. rice miso

- Wash and drain oats and roast in a hot, dry skillet until golden.
- Boil water and add oats and vegetables.
- Return to a boil and simmer 1 hour.
- Dilute miso in a little water, stir in, and simmer for 5 minutes.

SESAME-SHISO-NORI CONDIMENT

2 tsp. shiso leaves, minced and dry roasted, or 1 tsp. dry powdered shiso
1/4 cup roasted sesame seeds (brown or black)
2 Tbs. green nori flakes (*ao nori*)

• Grind shiso in a suribachi, add seeds and nori, and grind together until almost all the seeds are crushed.

APPLE FRITTERS

1 cooking apple, grated
1/2 cup cornmeal
a pinch of sea salt
pastry flour
corn oil

• Mix apple, cornmeal, and salt, adding just enough pastry flour to make them hold together.
• Heat a skillet and brush with oil.
• Form small balls with the batter, place on the skillet, flatten, and cook on both sides until golden.
• Serve as is or with a little heated rice syrup or barley malt.

Lunch

Seitan Sandwiches
Leftover Soup
Homemade Seitan

SEITAN SANDWICHES

whole grain bread, sliced
seitan, cut into slices
cucumber brine pickles or sauerkraut, sliced
red onion, thinly sliced
natural prepared mustard
corn oil

• Heat a skillet, brush with oil, and fry seitan slices on both sides until lightly crisp.
• Let seitan cool or serve hot. Put sandwiches together with choice of ingredients.

LEFTOVER SOUP

1 cup millet soup
$1/4$ cup leftover vegetables and tofu
extra water
raw garnish

• Mix leftovers, add water to desired consistency, simmer for 15 minutes, garnish, and serve

HOMEMADE SEITAN

4 cups hard spring or hard red winter wheat flour
$1/4$ cup 100% gluten flour (if available)
cold water and warm water
2-inch strip of kombu
several shiitake mushrooms
several slices of ginger
shoyu

• Put flour in a large bowl and mix well (yield is bigger when using gluten flour).

- Slowly mix in warm water until dough holds together and can be kneaded.
- Knead for 10 minutes or until firm. The more you knead it, the better it will come out.
- Cover with warm water and let sit at least 20 minutes, the longer the better but not too long so that the water sours.
- Knead in soaking water for 5 minutes. Water should become very clouded.
- Drain though a large, fine mesh strainer to remove the bran. Save bran and save liquid.
- Pour cold water over dough and knead in water for a few minutes. Drain off liquid as previously.
- Repeat with warm water, then cold water, continuing until almost all of the starch and bran are kneaded out, ending with cold water. The dough should be very elastic.
- Separate dough into small balls and rinse each under running water, pulling dough apart and kneading back together to remove any remaining starch and bran.
- Boil a large pot of water, drop seitan in, and boil until pieces float to the top. Stir once in a while to prevent sticking on the bottom.
- Remove seitan pieces and rinse with cold water until cool.
- Use water that the seitan pieces were boiled in, and add kombu, shiitake, ginger, and shoyu.
- Bring to a boil and drop seitan pieces in. Simmer for 30 minutes.
- Store in cooking liquid. Use seitan in soups, stews, stir fries, etc. Use liquid, kombu, and shiitake in cooking also.
- Let kneading water sit until all starch (white) sinks to the bottom and then gently pour liquid into another pot.
- Kneading water can be saved and used for soup or cereal. The bran can be cooked into cereals or desserts and the starch used for thickening in place of arrowroot or kuzu.

Dinner

Rice Salad
Sweet Navy Beans
Pressed Salad
Sauteed Summer Squash
Greens
Nishime Vegetables

RICE SALAD

2 cups leftover rice
$1/2$ seitan, diced
$1/2$ cup fresh peas, steamed
$1/2$ cup corn kernels, steamed
1 Tbs. brown rice vinegar

• Mix all ingredients and cool.

SWEET NAVY BEANS

1 cup dried navy beans
1 tsp. sweet miso
1 Tbs. barley malt or brown rice syrup

• Prepare and cook beans as in great northern beans recipe (*see Day 4*), without vegetables.
• Add syrup when adding miso, simmer 5 minutes, and stir well.

PRESSED SALAD

1 cup bok choy, thinly sliced
$1/2$ cup carrot, finely grated
$1/2$ cup cucumber, thinly sliced
1 Tbs. umeboshi vinegar
toasted sunflower seeds

- Put carrot in a salad press, then bok choy, followed by the cucumber. Pour vinegar over vegetables.
- Secure lid and press for about 15 minutes.
- Strain off liquid and save for a dressing or to use in cooking.
- Sprinkle with seeds and serve at room temperature or cool.

SAUTEED SUMMER SQUASH

1 onion, sliced into half moons
1 1/2 cups summer squash, sliced
1/2 tsp. fresh or dried dill weed
1 Tbs. parsley, minced
1 Tbs. corn oil
1 tsp. umeboshi vinegar

- Heat oil in a skillet, sauté onions for 5 minutes, and add squash, dill, and umeboshi vinegar.
- Sauté for a few minutes until squash is done, soft but still a little crisp.
- Stir in parsley and serve.
- Try oregano instead of dill and olive oil instead of corn.
- Optional: In cold weather substitute thinly sliced winter squash.

Steam or quick boil some greens.

NISHIME VEGETABLES

1 4-inch piece of kombu, cut into thin strips
1/2 cup lotus root, sliced into thin rounds
1 or 2 carrots, cut into 1-inch-wide rounds
sea salt
shoyu

- Place kombu pieces in a heavy pot.
- Place lotus in pot on one side and carrots on the other side.
- Add 1 1/2 inches of water and sprinkle with a few grains of sea salt.

- Cover and bring to a boil, simmering for 20 minutes.
- Sprinkle with shoyu and simmer a few more minutes.
- Gently scoop into a serving dish.

Day 14

Breakfast

Sweet Rice with Whole Wheat Berries
Miso Soup with Greens
Shio-Nori Condiment
Lotus-Shiitake Tea

SWEET RICE WITH WHOLE WHEAT BERRIES

$3/4$ cup sweet rice
$1/4$ cup whole wheat berries
3 cups water
1-inch square of kombu

- Wash and soak grains overnight.
- Place kombu in a pressure cooker and put grains and soaking water on top.
- Secure lid and cook under pressure for 60 minutes.
- Stir well and serve.

MISO SOUP WITH GREENS

1 Tbs. dulse
1/4 cup leeks, sliced
1/4 cup string beans, thinly sliced
1/4 cup celery, thinly sliced
4 1/2 cups water
2 tsp. barley miso
2 kale leaves, cut up
1/2 tsp. fresh ginger juice
celery leaves or scallion, sliced for garnish

• Boil water.
• In another pot, layer cut up dulse, then leeks, celery, and finally string beans.
• Gently pour water in and simmer for 5 minutes.
• Add kale stems while simmering.
• Dilute miso, add miso and leaves, and simmer 3 minutes.
• Add ginger juice and serve with garnish.

SHIO-NORI CONDIMENT

5 sheets of nori, cut into squares
1/2 to 3/4 cup water
shoyu
ginger juice

• Place nori in a small saucepan and cover with water.
• Bring to a boil, cover, and simmer on a low flame until almost all of the water evaporates and the nori forms a thick paste, 20 to 30 minutes.
• Add several drops of shoyu and simmer for 3 minutes using a flame deflector.
• Add ginger juice at the end of the cooking time.
• Serve over grain or noodles and let cool before storing in a glass airtight container.

LOTUS-SHIITAKE TEA

Lotus root tea helps relieve lung congestion and upper respiratory problems. Shiitake helps relax a contracted or tense condition.

$1/2$ cup fresh lotus root or a few small pieces of dried lotus root
1 small shiitake mushroom, rinsed and soaked until soft
shoyu

- *With fresh lotus root:* Wash lotus root and grate $1/2$ cup. Place pulp in a piece of cheesecloth and squeeze out the juice. Place the juice in a saucepan with an equal amount of water from soaking shiitake and cut up shiitake pieces. Add a few drops of shoyu and boil. Simmer for a few minutes. You may add a few drops of ginger juice at the end.

- *With dry lotus root:* Place a few small pieces of dried lotus root in a cup of water and let sit until soft enough to cut. Cut up into fine pieces and cut up shiitake. Cook lotus and shiitake in the soaking water with a few drops of shoyu. Bring to a boil and simmer for 15 minutes. Strain the liquid and drink while hot with ginger juice.

- *With lotus root power:* Use 1 level teaspoon of powder per cup, and dissolve in water. Heat on a low flame with shoyu for a a few minutes but do not boil. Ginger juice may be added.

Lunch

Tofu Lasagna
Garlic Bread
Onion Soup
Daikon and Greens

TOFU LASAGNA

½ lb. dried lasagna noodles
1 lb. soft tofu
1 Tbs. tahini
1 Tbs. umeboshi paste
1 clove garlic
1 cup carrots
1 cup parsnips
2 onions
½ lb. mochi, grated
¼ cup parsley, minced
1 tsp. sweet miso
oregano and basil

- Slightly undercook noodles and leave in water.
- Mash tofu and mix in tahini, umeboshi, mashed garlic, and miso. Heat for a few minutes on a low flame with mochi until mochi melts. Stir in parsley.
- Steam onions, parsnips, and carrots. Blend together, adding some of the steaming water for desired consistency. Add a little oregano and basil and simmer for a few minutes.
- Place a layer of noodles in a baking dish, spread tofu over, and continue until everything is used up, ending with noodles on top.
- Spread blended vegetables (sauce) over noodles and serve. Cut up pieces of seitan can be added to sauce.

GARLIC BREAD

slices of sourdough whole wheat bread
olive oil
garlic
sea salt

- Mix a little sea salt in some olive oil and heat on a very low flame, using a flame deflector, for 5 minutes.
- Slice or mash garlic, add to oil, and simmer for a few minutes.

- Brush both sides of bread with oil mixture and serve, or heat in a covered skillet on top of the stove or in a covered pan in the oven.

ONION SOUP

4 cups onions, thinly sliced
1 3- to 4-inch piece of kombu, cleaned, soaked, and sliced into thin matchsticks
3 to 4 shiitake mushrooms, soaked and sliced into thin pieces
5 to 6 cups water
toasted sesame oil
a pinch of sea salt
1 to 2 Tbs. shoyu
deep-fried whole wheat bread cubes (optional)
scallions, sliced for garnish

- Place kombu and shiitake (including soaking water from shiitake) in water and boil and simmer for 10 minutes.
- Heat a skillet, adding a generous amount of oil.
- Sauté onions and salt until they are very dark brown. Add shoyu and sauté on a low flame for 5 minutes.
- Add onions to water and simmer for 15 minutes.
- Garnish with bread cubes and scallions.

DAIKON AND GREENS

1 cup daikon, thinly sliced
1 cup daikon greens, sliced (use turnip or mustard greens if unavailable)

- Cook daikon using quick boiling method and place in the center of a large serving platter.
- Quickly cook greens the same way and place them around the daikon pieces.
- Optional: sprinkle with brown rice or umeboshi vinegar.

Dinner

Seitan with Apricot Sauce
Steamed Root Vegetables
Greens
Amasake Smoothie

SEITAN WITH APRICOT SAUCE

8 thick slices of prepared seitan
$1/2$ orange rind, grated
$1/2$ lemon rind, grated (use organic fruit and grate on large holes of a hand grater)
$1/2$ cup unsulphered apricots
3 cups water
a pinch of sea salt
a pinch of cinnamon (optional)
2 Tbs. rice syrup or barley malt

- Simmer water, apricots, salt, cinnamon, and rinds for half an hour.
- Purée in a blender or food mill.
- Mix in rice syrup and simmer a few more minutes.
- Place seitan in a baking dish and pour sauce over the pieces. Bake uncovered in a preheated 350 degree oven for 15 minutes, or heat together in a saucepan on top of the stove over a low flame.
- Serve as is or over boiled rice or noodles.

STEAMED ROOT VEGETABLES

carrots, onions, turnips, or rutabagas, cut into small pieces

- Steam each vegetable separately until done. Mix vegetables to serve.

GREENS

• Quick cook some light greens.

Heating leftovers: Leftovers that are dry can be reheated in a steamer basket.
• A few different leftovers can be combined to make a soup, salad, stir fry, or casserole.
• Some leftovers can be served cool or at room temperature such as pressed salad.

AMASAKE SMOOTHIE

2 cups prepared amasake
$1/2$ cup strawberries or blueberries

• Blend amasake and berries in a blender or food mill and serve as is or chilled
• Garnish with a fresh mint leaf or slice of lemon.

Resources

The One Peaceful World Society is an international information network and macrobiotic friendship society founded by Michio Kushi. Membership is $30/year for individuals ($40 outside of the U.S. and Canada) and $50 for families, and benefits include the quarterly *One Peaceful World Journal*, free books from One Peaceful World Press, and discounts on books and study materials. To join or for information, please contact One Peaceful World, Box 10, Becket, MA 01223, (413) 623-2322, Fax (413) 623-6042, e-mail opw@macrobiotics.org, website: www. macrobiotics.org

The Kushi Institute is an educational center for macrobiotic and holistic studies. For information on programs, including cooking seminars with Diane Avoli, please contact Kushi Institute, Box 7, Becket, MA 01223, (413) 623-5741, Fax (413) 623-8827, e-mail kushi@macrobiotics.org, website www. macrobiotics.org

About the Author

Diane Avoli has a background in special education and has been practicing and studying macrobiotics since 1971. She is the mother of eight and grandmother of two children. She teaches at the Kushi Institute and travels, offering cooking classes, counseling, and lectures.

Diane especially enjoys sharing experiences and ideas related to women's health issues, raising children, and family counseling.

Diane does phone consultations. She can be reached at P.O. Box 18, East Templeton, MA 01438, telephone (978) 632-8112.

Recipe Index

Aduki Soup, 43
Aduki-Kombu-Squash, 39
Amasake Smoothie, 92
Apple Fritters, 81
Arame with Vegetables, 21
Baked Squash and Onions, 34
Baked Tofu, 62
Bancha Tea, 24
Barley Stew, 56
Barley Stew with Croutons, 60
Barley Tea, 36
Bean Spread, 77
Blanched Bok Choy, 10
Boiled Basmati and Wild Rice, 66
Boiled Long-Grain Rice, 26
Boiled Mustard Greens, 18
Boiled Salad, 57
Bok Choy Stir Fry, 28
Broccoli Rabi, 30
Broccoli Soup, 32
Bulgur with Wakame, 61
Carrot Soup, 60
Chickpea Sauce, 33
Chickpeas and Fu, 27
Collard Greens, 21
Corn Grits, 75
Corn on the Cob, 71
Cornbread, 64
Creamed Cauliflower Soup, 38
Crepes, 53
Cucumber Pickles, 25
Daikon and Greens, 90
Daikon Nishimi and Greens, 33
Deep Fried Tofu, 11
Double Cooked String Beans, 62
Dulse Miso Soup, 16
Fried Couscous, 36
Fried Rice, 18

Garlic Bread, 89
Gomashio, 22
Goma-Wakame Condiment, 80
Great Northern Beans, 72
Green Rolls, 73
Greens, 92
Herb Dressing, 67
Hiziki with Dried Daikon and Leeks, 73
Homemade Rice Kayu Bread, 69
Homemade Seitan, 82
Homemade Sprouts, 77
Kidney Bean Soup, 20
Kidney Beans with Onions, 14
Kinpira, 20
Kombu Broth (Daishi), 11
Layered Miso Soup, 75
Leftover Soup, 82
Leftover Veggies, 37
Lemon Rice Syrup Sauce, 35
Lemon-Miso Sauce, 62
Lentil Patties, 48
Lentil Stew, 44
Lotus-Shiitake Tea, 88
Marinated Cucumbers, 48
Medium Grain Rice with Whole Oats, 19
Millet Loaf, 71
Millet Soup, 78
Millet with Onions, 38
Millet with Squash or Corn, 13
Miso-Lemon Sauce, 62
Miso Soup, 9, 41, 47, 63
Miso Soup with Fried Mochi, 30
Miso Soup with Greens, 87
Miso Soup with Shredded Kombu, 52
Miso-Tahini Sauce, 70

Mochi Pancakes, 47
Natto Soybeans, 65
Nishime Style Vegetables, 14
Nishimi Vegetables, 85
Nishimi with Kuzu Sauce, 18
Noodle Rolls, 42
Nori Condiment, 42
Nori Rolls, 59
Nutty Rice, 78
Oatmeal with Raisins, 10
Onion Butter, 68
Onion Soup, 90
Pasta Salad, 31, 76
Pasta Sauce, 31
Pasta with String Beans, 65
Pickled Collard Stems, 74
Pressed Cucumbers, 40
Pressed Nappa and Bean Sprouts, 55
Pressed Salad, 28, 84
Pressure-Cooked Short Grain Brown Rice, 13
Pumpkin Seed Condiment, 15
Quick Boiled Greens, 46
Quick Onion Pickles, 36
Quick Pressed Pickles, 68
Quick Stir Fry, 43
Raw Salad, 67
Red Radish Umeboshi Pickles, 46
Rice Pudding, 49
Rice Salad, 84
Rice with Black Soybeans, 55
Sandwich Spread, 25
Sautéed Cabbage, 56
Sautéed Kale, 15
Sautéed Summer Squash, 85
Sautéed Vegetables, 45
Scallion-Miso Condiment, 40
Scrambled Tofu, 63
Sea Palm, 45
Sea Palm Salad, 48
Seitan Sandwiches, 82
Seitan with Apricot Sauce, 91
Sesame Umeboshi Dressing, 76
Sesame-Shio-Nori Condiment, 81

Shiitake-Scallion Broth with Instant Kombu, 50
Shio-Nori Condiment, 87
Shoyu and Vinegar Pickles, 29
Shoyu Soup, 58
Soba Noodles, 49
Soft Barley with Vegetables, 58
Soft Millet, 16
Soft Millet and Onions, 41
Soft Sweet Rice and Oats with Dried Fruit, 23
Somen Noodles, 11
Sourdough Pancakes, 35
Squash Kanten, 79
Squash Sauce, 72
Squash with Wakame, 57
Steamed Bread, 68
Steamed Broccoli, 17, 39
Steamed Greens, 23, 53
Steamed Pea Pods, 58
Steamed Rice, 33
Steamed Rice Kayu Bread, 69
Steamed Root Vegetables, 91
Stir Fry Vegetables with Tofu, 79
Stuffed Cabbage, 70
Sweet Navy Beans, 84
Sweet Rice with Chestnuts, 44
Sweet Rice with Whole Wheat Berries, 86
Sweet Vegetable Drink, 31
Tempuraed Vegetables with Dip, 50
Tofu Dressing, 57
Tofu Lasagna, 89
Tofu Sandwiches, 24
Vegetable Stew, 27, 61
Vegetable Topping, 54
Watercress, 12, 60
Water-Sautéed Onions and Carrots, 66
Water-Sautéed Nappa, 75
White Fish, 66
Whole Barley with Sweet Rice, 29
Whole Oats with Vegetables, 80
Whole Wheat Couscous Cereal, 52